PHILIPPIANS

NCCS | New Covenant Commentary Series

The New Covenant Commentary Series (NCCS) is designed for ministers and students who require a commentary that interacts with the text and context of each New Testament book and pays specific attention to the impact of the text upon the faith and praxis of contemporary faith communities.

The NCCS has a number of distinguishing features. First, the contributors come from a diverse array of backgrounds in regards to their Christian denominations and countries of origin. Unlike many commentary series that tout themselves as international the NCCS can truly boast of a genuinely international cast of contributors with authors drawn from every continent of the world (except Antarctica) including countries such as the United States, Australia, the United Kingdom, Kenya, India, Singapore, and Korea. We intend the NCCS to engage in the task of biblical interpretation and theological reflection from the perspective of the global church. Second, the volumes in this series are not verse-by-verse commentaries, but they focus on larger units of text in order to explicate and interpret the story in the text as opposed to some often atomistic approaches. Third, a further aim of these volumes is to provide an occasion for authors to reflect on how the New Testament impacts the life, faith, ministry, and witness of the New Covenant Community today. This occurs periodically under the heading of "Fusing the Horizons and Forming the Community." Here authors provide windows into community formation (how the text shapes the mission and character of the believing community) and ministerial formation (how the text shapes the ministry of Christian leaders).

It is our hope that these volumes will represent serious engagements with the New Testament writings, done in the context of faith, in service of the church, and for the glorification of God.

Series Editors:

Michael F. Bird (Ridley College, Parkville, VIC, Australia)

Craig Keener (Asbury Theological Seminary, Wilmore, KY, USA)

Titles in this series:

Mark Kim Huat Tan

Luke Diane Chen

John Jey J. Kanagaraj

Acts Youngmo Cho and Hyung Dae Park

Romans Craig Keener

1 Corinthians B. J. Oropeza

Galatians Jarvis J. Williams

Ephesians Lynn Cohick

Philippians Linda L. Belleville

Colossians and Philemon Michael F. Bird

1–2 Thessalonians Nijay K. Gupta

1 Timothy Aída Besançon-Spencer

2 Timothy and Titus Aída Besançon-Spencer

The Epistle of John Samuel M. Ngewa

Jude and 2 Peter Andrew Mbuvi

Revelation Gordon Fee

Forthcoming titles:

Matthew Catherine Sider-Hamilton

2 Corinthians J. Ayodeji Adewuya

Hebrews Cynthia Long Westfall

James Ruth Anne Reese

1 Peter Sean du Toit

PHILIPPIANS

A New Covenant Commentary

Linda L. Belleville

CASCADE *Books* · Eugene, Oregon

PHILIPPIANS
A New Covenant Commentary

New Covenant Commentary Series

Copyright © 2021 Linda L. Belleville. All rights reserved. Except for brief quotations in critical publications or reviews, no part of this book may be reproduced in any manner without prior written permission from the publisher. Write: Permissions, Wipf and Stock Publishers, 199 W. 8th Ave., Suite 3, Eugene, OR 97401.

Cascade Books
An Imprint of Wipf and Stock Publishers
199 W. 8th Ave., Suite 3
Eugene, OR 97401

www.wipfandstock.com

PAPERBACK ISBN: 978-1-60899-041-2
HARDCOVER ISBN: 978-1-4982-8488-2
EBOOK ISBN: 978-1-4982-4120-5

Cataloguing-in-Publication data:

Names: Belleville, Linda L., author

Title: Philippians : a new covenant commentary / by Linda L. Belleville.

Description: Eugene, OR: Cascade Books, 2021. | Series: A New Covenant Commentary | Includes bibliographical references.

Identifiers: ISBN 978-1-60899-041-2 (paperback) | ISBN 978-1-4982-8488-2 (hardcover) | ISBN 978-1-4982-4120-5 (ebook)

Subjects: LCSH: Bible. Philippians—Commentaries.

Classification: BS2705.53 B45 2021 (paperback) | BS2705.53 (ebook)

03/04/21

To my mentor and model of grace and generosity Richard N. Longenecker

CONTENTS

AUTHOR'S PREFACE

I welcome the opportunity to express my appreciation to Mike Bird and Craig Keener for their gracious invitation to write a commentary on a Pauline letter that has been a favorite one, since my days on staff with InterVarsity Christian Fellowship forty years ago. It has been a joy to consider the content and relevance of Paul's most personal of missives for Christian living in today's global church and society.

I am also very grateful for the generous extensions I received due to both teaching and family circumstances from the editors for Cascade Books. In my research and writing, I find that God makes the project much more than an academic piece. The challenges that Paul faced in addressing problems in his churches become personal challenges for me as well. The theme of Philippians is that of "joy" and Paul's call for the Philippian church to always rejoice despite the circumstances became a personal challenge for me as well:

> Continue to rejoice in the Lord always. Again I say rejoice. Let your restraint be known to all people. The Lord is near. Stop being anxious for anyhing but in everything with prayer and petition with thanksgiving, let your requests be made known to God. God's peace, which surpasses all understanding, will guard your hearts and minds in Christ Jesus. (4:4–7)

Deo gratias

ABBREVIATIONS

BOOKS

AB	Anchor Bible
ABD	The Anchor Bible Dictionary
ACCS	Ancient Christian Commentary on Scripture
AnBib	Analecta biblica
Anlex	Analytical Lexicon of the Greek New Testament
ANTC	Abingdon New Testament Commentaries
BDAG	A Greek-English Lexicon of the New Testament
BDF	A Greek Grammar of the New Testament
BECNT	Baker Exegetical Commentary on the New Testament
BGBE	Beiträge zur Geschichte der biblischen Exegese
BNTC	Black's New Testament Commentaries
BTCB	Brazos Theological Commentary on the Bible
BZNW	Beihefte zur ZNW
ConBNT	Coniectanea biblica, New Testament
EB	Encyclopedia Britannica
EBC	Expositor's Bible Commentary
ECC	Eerdmans Critical Commentary
HNTC	Harper's New Testament Commentaries
HTS	Harvard Theological Studies
IBC	International Biblical Commentary
ICC	International Critical Commentary

WBC   Word Biblical Commentary

WUNT   Wissenschaftliche Untersuchungen zum Neuen Testament

JOURNALS

AJA	*American Journal of Archaeology*
AsTJ	*Asbury Theological Journal*
ATJ	*Ashland Theological Journal*
ATR	*Anglican Theological Review*
BA	*Biblical Archaeologist*
BASOR	*Bulletin of the American Schools of Oriental Research*
BBR	*Bulletin for Biblical Research*
Bib	*Biblica*
BibInt	*Biblical Interpretation*
BJRL	*Bulletin of the John Rylands University Library of Manchester*
BK	*Bibel und Kirche*
BR	*Biblical Research*
BRev	*Bible Review*
BSac	*Bibliotheca Sacra*
BTB	*Biblical Theology Bulletin*
BW	*Biblical World*
BZ	*Biblische Zeitschrift*
CBQ	*Catholic Biblical Quarterly*
CRBS	*Currents in Research, Biblical Studies*
CSR	*Christian Scholars Review*
CTJ	*Calvin Theological Journal*
CTR	*Concordia Theological Review*
DC	*Doctor Communis*
EvQ	*Evangelical Quarterly*

ExpTim	*Expository Times*
HBT	*Horizons in Biblical Theology*
HTR	*Harvard Theological Review*
Int	*Interpretation*
JAAR	*Journal of the American Academy of Religion*
JBL	*Journal of Biblical Literature*
JETS	*Journal of the Evangelical Theological Society*
JHC	*Journal of Higher Criticism*
JJS	*Journal of Jewish Studies*
JNES	*Journal of Near Eastern Studies*
JQR	*Jewish Quarterly Review*
JR	*Journal of Religion*
JRS	*Journal of Roman Studies*
JSNT	*Journal for the Study of the New Testament*
JSOT	*Journal for the Study of the Old Testament*
JTS	*Journal of Theological Studies*
JTC	*Journal for Theology and the Church*
LQ	*Lutheran Quarterly*
NovT	*Novum Testamentum*
NTS	*New Testament Studies*
PSB	*Princeton Seminary Bulletin*
RB	*Revue biblique*
RevExp	*Review and Expositor*
ResQ	*Restoration Quarterly*
RSR	*Recherches de science religieuse*
SJT	*Scottish Journal of Theology*
TrinJ	*Trinity Journal*
TLZ	*Theologische Literaturzeitung*
TS	*Theological Studies*
TU	*Texte und Untersuchungen*

TynBul	Tyndale Bulletin
TZ	Theologische Zeitschrift
VE	Vox Evangelica
VT	Vetus Testamentum
WTJ	Wesminster Theological Journal
ZAW	Zeitschrift für die altestamentliche Wissenschaft
ZNW	Zeitschrift für die neutestamentliche Wissenschaft

Introduction to Philippians

The City of Philippi

Luke refers to Philippi as "the leading city of the district of Macedonia" (Acts 16:12). The province of Macedonia was divided into four districts with each district having a leading city. Philippi was a strategic city for the Romans. It had the prestigious title "Colony of Julius Augusta Philippi *ius Italicum*," which was a most coveted title. *Ius Italicum* meant it was part of Italy and considered a Roman city with all the rights and privileges as such. It was exempt from paying taxes, had the right of land ownership, full civic rights, and its own administrators: *strategoi* "magistrates" (v. 22) and *lictores* "police sergeants" (v. 35; versus Roman appointed officials).[1]

The city was named after Philip II of Macedon (Alexander the Great's father), who took the city from the Thracians in 360 BC. He united all the city-states in northern Greece under his centralized control and formed the province of "Macedonia." The leading city, Philippi, was his namesake.[2]

Although rich in minerals, Philippi's ten-mile distance from the port of Neapolis lowered the city's commercial importance.[3] Philippi's renown came from the battles fought there. In 42 BC the imperial armies of Octavian and Antony fought and beat Brutus and Cassius. In 31 BC Octavian fought and beat Antony and Cleopatra. Soldiers from Octavian's army settled there to stabilize the area.

---

1. Lemerle 1945: 7–10. The NRSV is cited unless otherwise indicated.
2. van der Crabben 2009: "Philippi."
3. Strabo, *Geogr.* 7.331.

Founding Visit

While in Troas, Paul had a vision of a man from Macedonia asking for help (Acts 16:11–40). Luke recounts: "When he [Paul] had seen the vision, we immediately tried to cross over to Macedonia, being convinced that God had called us to proclaim the good news to them." The fact that Luke shifts from "he" to "we" at this point indicates that Paul met Luke in Troas. Luke reverts back to "he," once Paul moves on to Thessalonica (Acts 17). The fact that Luke stayed on at Philippi points to the city being Luke's hometown. As a doctor, this makes sense, since Philippi had a famous school of medicine with graduates throughout the Roman Empire.

Paul's travel to Macedonia marks the advance of the gospel into Europe. His missionary strategy emerged once he heeded the Macedonian man's call for help. Macedonia was about 10,000 square miles or roughly the size of Maryland. Therefore, some kind of strategic planning was needed. Acts 16–20 shows Paul's development of a three-pronged strategy. The first step was to identify the area's major urban center, which would allow for maximum evangelistic impact. When Paul moved on, he entrusted the spread of the gospel into surrounding areas to his urban converts (e.g., Epaphras and Colossae; Col 1:7; 4:12).

Paul's second step was the local synagogue (Acts 13:5, 14; 14:1; 17:2, 10, 17; 18:4, 19; 19:8).[4] There he would find the most prepared audience, including both the pious Jew and Gentile "God-Fearers."[5] This also accords with Paul's policy of "to the Jew first." As God's chosen people historically, the Jews had a right to hear the gospel first (Rom 1:15). Paul's third step was to concentrate on the family unit as the nucleus of the church (e.g., 1 Cor 16:15). His letters commonly include greetings to the church that meets in a particular person's home (Rom 16:3, 5; 1 Cor 16:19; Col 4:15; Phlm 2). This "household" church became Paul's base of operation and effective means of spreading the gospel. A "home" in Paul's day included more than immediate

---

4. The local synagogue was Paul's focus even before his call to Macedonia. As a visiting rabbi, he would automatically be asked to speak. The synagogue's leadership was in the hands of an administrator referred to as "ruler of the synagogue." The pastoral rabbi is a modern phenomena. There also were no religious elders to be found in the local synagogue. Elders in both Gentile and Jewish circles functioned as civic leaders.

5. The term "God-fearers" is used of non-Jews who attended the local synagogue and followed Jewish Law except for circumcision.

family members. Extended family, staff and frequent visitors resulted in a "household" that was comparable to the aristocratic estates of Europe.[6]

This three-pronged strategy is found in Acts 16:11–15. Philippi was "the leading city of its Macedonian district" (v. 12). On arriving in Philippi, Paul learned that Jews gathered for worship near a river. Jewish law required the presence of ten male heads of households to form a synagogue. Lacking that, a place of prayer under the open sky and near a body of water was chosen. Luke notes, "On the Sabbath day we went outside the gate by the river, where we supposed there was a place of prayer; and we sat down and spoke to the women who had gathered there" (v. 13). It was there that a woman named Lydia, a worshiper of God, responded to the gospel message and invited the mission party to make her home their headquarters: "If you have judged me to be faithful to the Lord, come and stay at my home" (v. 15). The household of Lydia became the nucleus for the Philippian church. Lydia was a prominent Jewish business woman of financial means. She was from the city of Thyatira and a dealer in purple cloth (v. 14). The impact of her friendship and generosity on Paul can be seen from the fact that the church at Philippi was the only church from which Paul accepted personal support (Phil 4:15).

The Importance of Roman Citizenship

Barnabas, Paul's companion during their first evangelistic endeavor, had a parting of ways over John Mark's defection after evangelistic efforts on Cyprus (Acts 15:36–40). In his place, Paul chose Silas (Roman name Silvanus). Silas and Judas were selected as the Jerusalem church's representatives to return with Paul and Barnabas to the Gentile church at Antioch with the Jerusalem Council decree (Acts 15:27). Luke notes that Silas and Judas were prophets, who did much to encourage and strengthen the Antiochian believers (Acts 15:32). Luke further notes that Silas like Paul was a Roman citizen (Acts 16:37). Among other benefits, Roman citizenship provided protection against interference by local authorities.

Paul and Silas went through Syria and Cilicia, delivering the Council's decree and strengthening the churches (Acts 15:41). They also went to Derbe and to Lystra, where they met a convert named Timothy, whose mother was a Jewish believer and whose father was Greek. Because Timothy was highly recommended by both Lystra and Iconium believers, Paul

6. Martin 1996: 40–60.

added him to the team after he was circumcised (16:1–6).[7] It was the "trio" of Paul, Silas, and Timothy who set off for missionary work in Macedonia.

While in Philippi, Paul and Silas encountered strong opposition. Paul exorcised a demon from a slave girl, who had a spirit of divination that brought her owners a great deal of money by fortune-telling. The Greek is literally "the spirit of the Python" (*pneuma pythōna* Acts 16:16). According to the Greek myth, the Python was the serpent that inspired and guarded the oracle at Delphi. Although the creature was slain by the god Apollo, belief in a divining spirit remained.[8] The slave girl through her demonic spirit had insight into the identity and mission of Paul and his company: "These men are servants of the Most High God, who proclaim to you the way of salvation" (v. 17). At some point Paul became annoyed enough to command the spirit in the name of Jesus Christ to come out of her, and it did.[9] Her owners realizing that they had lost their means of financial gain, seized Paul and Si- las and dragged them before the local magistrates, claiming, "these men are Jews, who were disturbing the peace by advocating customs that are not lawful for the Roman citizens of Philippi to adopt or observe" (vv. 21–22). Their intent was to play on the anti-Semitism of the city and Philippi's pride in being a free Roman city. Although Judaism was an officially sanctioned religion, the lack of a synagogue (visible Jewish presence) combined with Philippi's status as a Roman city with autonomous governance put Paul and Silas at great risk. Even so, their Roman citizenship would have protected them. A Roman citizen could not be falsely charged, beaten, or jailed. Due process also required a fair trial with the right of appeal to Caesar.

However, neither Paul nor Silas claimed these rights. Instead the crowd joined in attacking them and the magistrates had them stripped of their clothing and ordered them to be beaten with rods (Acts 16:31). Afterwards

7. Luke's mention that Timothy's father was Greek explains why he was not circumcised. The fact that his mother was Jewish meant that in the eyes of society, Timothy was neither Jew nor Greek and would therefore not be accepted in either context. Circumcision normalized his social standing as a "Jew." This was critical for missionary work. Paul's policy of seeking out a synagogue in each city to which he went meant that Timothy would be accepted as a Jew. Jew-Gentile marriages were so rare that Timothy's situation would be well-known in his social circles. Luke states: "Paul wanted Timothy to accompany him; and he took him and had him circumcised because of the Jews who were in those places, for they all knew that his father was a Greek" (Acts 16:30).

8. O'Toole 1996: 58.

9. Although some scholars view this record as unhistorical, there are others who defend the account in the light of Paul's own statements about his miraculous accomplishments (Rom 15:18–19; 2 Cor 12:11–13). See Lüdemann 1989: 189–91.

they were jailed, put in the innermost cell, and their feet fastened in the stocks (v. 32). Only at daybreak, when the city magistrates sent their police officers to release them with the order to go in peace, does Paul invoke Roman citizenship: "They have beaten us in public, uncondemned men who are Roman citizens, and have thrown us into prison; and now are they going to discharge us in secret? Certainly not! Let them [the magistrates] come and take us out themselves" (v. 37). Luke notes that the magistrates "were afraid," when they heard that they were Roman citizens (vv. 38–39). So they came and apologized to them. Then they released them and asked them to leave the city (v. 39).

Opinions vary on why Paul waited to declare his Roman citizenship. A reasonable explanation can be found in the anti-Semitism and autonomy of Philippi. The fledgling church could be persecuted as an unauthorized gathering of those engaging in illegal, non-Roman practices. Paul and Silas guaranteed the church's protection. As long as Paul and Silas did not report their abuse as Roman citizens, the local magistrates would be indebted to them. Both beating and jailing a Roman citizen were serious offenses. Roman citizenship was a great privilege not easily obtained and the consequences were severe. Philippi's status as a Roman city could be removed and a Roman governor sent to replace the magistrates. Paul's and Silas's actions meant that the local magistrates would be slow to move against the church in the near future.

Paul's Situation

Paul's situation at the time of writing is clearly stated. He is in prison awaiting trial: "I want you to know, beloved, that what has happened to me has actually helped to spread the gospel so that it has become known throughout the whole praetorian [imperial] guard and to everyone else that my imprisonment is for Christ" (Phil 1:12–13). He speaks of the outcome being life or death: "Christ will be exalted now as always in my body, whether by life or by death" (1:20). He anticipates that the outcome will be life and that he will come visit them. This is based on the conviction that God has more work for him to do: "Since I am convinced of this, I know that I will remain and continue with all of you for your progress and joy in faith, so that I may share abundantly in your boasting in Christ Jesus, when I come to you again" (1:25–26).

The location and date of Paul's imprisonment has been debated. Traditionally the letter has been dated c. AD 61–62 and written in Rome. There is much to commend a Roman provenance. Mention of the "praetorian guard" fits with Rome (Phil 1:12–13).[10] "*We* sailed from Philippi" (Acts 20:6) indicates that Luke joined the Jerusalem collection's representatives at this point. "We" is also found during Paul's appeal to be tried in Caesar's court (which was his right as a Roman citizen) and during Paul's trip from Caesarea to Rome (Acts 27–28). Luke records that on arriving in Rome, Paul was a prisoner under house arrest (*custodia libera*) for about two years (Acts 28:30–31). He had a soldier guarding him (28:16), but he was free to send letters, to receive visitors, and to preach the gospel (vv. 17, 30–31). Paul's situation in Philippians of "imprisonment" indicates that he was moved to a place of confinement (perhaps in the barracks of the Praetorian Guard) and that his trial had begun ("in my defense" Phil 1:7). The fact that the verdict will be either life or death supports a trial before Caesar in Rome. Paul states that the entire imperial guard knew that he was in prison because of Christ (v. 13). Greetings are sent from believers in Caesar's household (4:22).[11] This would place Philippians after the writing of Colossians and Philemon. Paul's situation in Colossians and Philemon fits the ending of Acts, where his colleagues are free to come and go. "Epaphras, Mark Aristarchus, Demas and Luke" send greetings (Phlm 23–24; Col 4:10–16). The support for a Roman imprisonment origin is thus substantial.[12]

Some scholars have challenged a Roman origin for Philippians and suggested Ephesus, Caesarea, or a second Roman imprisonment as alternatives. The primary difficulty is one of distance from Rome to Philippi, which is hard to reconcile with a quick trip for Timothy as the letter carrier (2:19) and the return of the church's recently ill emissary and gift carrier, Epaphroditus (Phil 2:25–30; 4:15–20).[13]

10. Tacitus, *Hist.* 4.46; Suetonius, *Nero* 9; MM 1929: 553.

11. The Roman household included extended family, servants, business associates, visitors, and those under the owner's patronage. Caesar's household undoubtedly would have been extensive. Numerous household slaves and servants were needed to run a Roman household. See Martin 1996: 40–60.

12. See, for example, Buchanan 1964: 157–66; Reicke 1970: 277–86; Johnson 1956: 24–26 and most modern commentaries.

13. See Collange 1979: 155. Compare Burton 1896: 46–56 and Cassidy 2001: Introduction.

In 1900 H. Lisco first suggested that Paul may have written his letter to the Philippians from Ephesus (c. AD 54–57).[14] Since then a number of scholars have followed his lead and supplemented his suggestion with detailed arguments.[15] An Ephesian provenance is based on Paul's information in 2 Corinthians that he and his colleagues had a near-death experience traveling through Asia from Ephesus to Troas (2 Cor 1:8–10). However, Paul does not mention an imprisonment as he does in the so-called Prison Letters (Ephesians, Colossians, Philemon). Also nothing in 2 Cor 1:8–10 supports the presence of an imperial guard in Ephesus or a trial. Further, the "we" language of 2 Corinthians means that Paul's colleague, Timothy, faced the same peril, while in Philippians, it is just Paul himself. Paul did face opposition in Ephesus from the local Artemis silversmiths, whose business was threatened, and they sought to stir up the crowd. However, the town clerk squashed the effort and pointed out that the courts are open and there are proconsuls to handle formal charges (Acts 19:38).

It is also argued that the imperial guard served as bodyguards for high-ranking officials such as a provincial governor. It is further noted that Timothy was with Paul in Ephesus (Acts 19:22; Phil 1:1) and that his projected trip to Philippi from Ephesus harmonizes with Luke's recorded itinerary in Acts (Phil 2:19; cf. Acts 19:22). However, historians have documented their presence only during the era of the Roman Republic. With the transition to imperial Rome, the imperial guard praetorians served only the emperor.[16]

Issue is taken as well with the fact that Paul appears not to have been back to Philippi since his founding visit c. AD 50 (Phil 1:30 and 4:15–16). He does anticipate visiting them again (Phil 1:26; 2:12, 22) and, indeed, Luke places Paul in Macedonia after he leaves Ephesus in c. AD 56 (Acts 20:2a). It is argued that this would place Philippians after his AD 50 founding visit (Acts 16) and prior to his AD 56 return to Macedonia (Acts 20). However, a visit to Philippi is not specifically mentioned by Luke. Paul's intent was to collect monies for the Jerusalem church from all his churches and then to set sail with the churches' representatives to Jerusalem. In fact, Paul tells the Corinthian church that he plans to visit them *after* passing

14. Lisco 1900.

15. Collange 1979: 155; Wood 1877: 229; McNeile 1955: 182n3. Duncan argued the case strongly in 1955–1956: 163–66.

16. See, Smith 1875: "Praetoriani."

through Macedonia and perhaps even spend the winter in Corinth (1 Cor 16:5–6).

Mention is made of the successful collection of monies from the Macedonian churches (plural) in his c. AD 56 letter to the Corinthian church (2 Cor 8:1–5) as well as his plan to visit Corinth and collect their monies as well (2 Cor 8–9). Luke does record such a Corinthian stay, where he states that Paul "stayed for three months" (Acts 20:3). Luke also mentions Paul's plan to sail with the monies from Greece to Jerusalem but that he was informed of a plot against him: "He was about to set sail for Syria when a plot was made against him by the Jews" (Act 20:3). Instead he returned to Macedonia and set sail from there with the Jerusalem collection and the churches' representatives: "And so he decided to return through Macedonia. He was accompanied by Sopater son of Pyrrhus from Beroea, by Aristarchus and Secundus from Thessalonica, by Gaius from Derbe, and by Timothy, as well as by Tychicus and Trophimus from Asia" (Acts 20:3–4). While at Corinth, Paul wrote to the Roman church about his plan after his Jerusalem visit to move into unchartered evangelistic territory west of Rome and perhaps as far as Spain (Rom 15:24–28). Caesarean (Acts 23–26) and Roman (Acts 27–28) imprisonments forestalled these plans. In Philippians, on the other hand, Paul anticipates a release from prison and speaks of further evangelistic work in Philippi (Phil 1:26). Plans can change. Five years passed between the writing of Romans (c. AD 57) and Paul's release from prison (c. AD 62). 1 Timothy and Titus indicate that Paul did not end up going west but returned east to engage in the further evangelistic work. This supports a c. AD 62 date for Philippians.

Caesarea is an attractive imprisonment option, given that Paul was held in the military barracks for two years.[17] Even so, Paul's mention of the Praetorian guard, an imprisonment, and a trial with a life or death verdict does not fit the account of events in Acts 23–26. Paul was taken from Jerusalem to Caesarea by the order of the military tribune for his protection against hostile Jews who sought to kill him (Acts 23:16–24). The charges brought by the Jews were dismissed as a sectarian religious matter. The centurion who transported him was ordered by Felix the procurator to keep Paul in custody but to let him have some liberty and not prevent any of his friends from taking care of his needs (Acts 24:23). When Felix learned that Paul was a Roman citizen (assuming wealth), he held him for two years

---

17. A Caesarean provenance for Philippians was first proposed by Heinrich E. G. Paulus in 1799. See also Johnson 1956–1957: 24–26 and Reicke 1970: 277–86.

hoping that Paul would bribe him. Wanting to curry favor with his Jewish subjects, Festus, Felix's successor, agreed to have Paul sent back to Jerusalem for trial. It is at this point that Paul appealed to his right as a Roman citizen to be tried before Caesar (Acts 25:10–12).

More recently Jim Reiher has proposed a second Roman imprisonment as the provenance of Philippians. Similarities between Philippians and 2 Timothy are noted. It is argued that an advanced ecclesiology, an impending sense of death, the mention of Luke, the word *desmios* regarding imprisonment (versus simply house arrest) and a desertion of co-workers are found only in Philippians and 2 Timothy.[18]

Yet, while the proposal is appealing, the similarities are overstated. In Philippians, Paul anticipates a release and return to Philippi versus a death verdict (Phil 1:25). To be sure, there is a lack of unity among the leadership (Phil 4:3). Yet, there are no deserting colleagues as one finds in 2 Timothy: "All who are in Asia have turned away from me, including Phygelus and Hermogenes" (1:15). "Demas has deserted me" (4:10). Paul does address the Philippian "overseers and deacons" (1:1). However, this is not a sign of an advanced ecclesiology. The terms "overseer" and "deacon" appear earlier in Paul's letters. Phoebe is identified as a deacon at the Cenchrean church (Rom 16:1). Also, the terms "overseer" and "elder" are not easily distinguished in Paul's letters. Paul appointed "elders" in all his churches to "oversee" spiritual matters (Acts 14:23). Nor are the terms "overseer" and "elder" easily distinguished even in 1 Timothy or Titus. In 1 Timothy the leadership is named as "overseers" (3:1) and "deacons" (3:8). In Titus, Paul commands him to appoint "elders" in all the towns, who are to "oversee" the churches that they planted (1:5–7). Further, the Greek word for imprisonment *desmios* is not unique to Philippians and 2 Timothy as Reiher claims. It is the term Paul also uses to describe his situation in Ephesians (3:1) and Philemon (1).

Integrity Issues

Three sections have been claimed by some to be insertions: (1) 2:6–11; (2) 2:19–24; and (3) 3:1b–19.[19]

---

18. Reiher 2012: 213–33.

19. See Dalton 1979: 97–102; Garland 1985: 141–73; Jewett 1970: 40–53.

Phil 2:6–11 has been regarded as an interpolation. The most common position is that these verses are an early Christian hymn cited by Paul at this point in the letter. (See the Excursus below.)

Phil 2:19–24 falls into the category of a travel narrative, which typically appears at the end of Greco-Roman letters. However, the concerns expressed in these verses could have prompted Paul to put it earlier. Paul announces the return of Epaphroditus but notes that his return has been delayed by a serious illness: "I think it necessary to send to you Epaphroditus—my brother and co-worker and fellow soldier, your messenger and minister to my needs. He was indeed so ill that he nearly died" (2:25–27). "Welcome him then in the Lord with all joy and honor such people, because he came close to death for the work of Christ, risking his life to make up for those services that you could not give me" (2:29). This sounds like a defense on behalf of Epaphroditus and very similar to what Paul says about Onesimus in Philemon. The Philippian church may have become worried at Epaphoriditus' delay as he was carrying funds for Paul (4:10–20). Carrying a large sum of money was always a concern. Highway robbery was quite common in Paul's day: "I have been in danger from rivers, in danger from bandits . . . in danger in the country" (2 Cor 11:26).[20]

Phil 3:1b–10 appears to be out of place with its so-called bitter severity and self-defense in light of the letter's overall theme of joy. Phil 3:1a begins with a *to loipon* commonly translated "finally": "Finally, my brothers and sisters, rejoice in the Lord. To write the same things to you is not troublesome to me, and for you it is a safeguard" (3:1 NRSV). The language of "writing" typically follows a notification of travel plans in the Greco-Roman letter. The outburst in Phil 3:1b: "Beware of the dogs; beware of the evil workers; beware of those who mutilate the flesh!" (NRSV) seems disconnected with what precedes. However, Paul's letters are notorious for abrupt changes. Virtually every letter has one or more such transitions. It could well be that Phil 3:1a marked a dictation pause or a letter disruption, during which time Paul learned of the arrival of Jewish agitators from Palestine intent on giving false evidence at his trial (or possibly at the hearing of his appeal).

---

20. 1 Corinthians is another example in which Paul attaches certain travel plans at the end of chapter 4 and the rest at the end of chapter 16. In chapter 1–4 Paul addresses itinerant preachers who are challenging his authority. He states that he "will come to [Corinth] soon, if the Lord wills, and I will find out not the talk of these arrogant people but their power" (v. 19).

Even more, rigid (word-for-word) English translations can misrepresent the Greek. First, *to loipon* is used by Paul elsewhere to mark a transition to another topic (e.g., "Now for the rest"). Paul's use includes "from now on, in the future, henceforth" (1 Cor 7:29; Gal 6:17; 2 Tim 4:8), "beyond that"; in addition" (1 Cor 1:16; 2 Cor 13:11; Phil 4:8; 1 Thess 4:1) and "furthermore" (1 Cor 4:2; BDAG s.v.). 1 Thess 4:1 is a case in point. Here *to loipon* introduces a change of topic: "In addition, brothers and sisters, we ask and urge you in the Lord Jesus that as you learned from us how you ought to live and to please God (as, in fact, you are doing), you should do so more and more" (NRSV). Yet, at verse 13 Paul moves on to still another topic: "We do not want you to be uninformed, brothers and sisters, about those who have died, so that you may not grieve as others do who have no hope." Similarly *to loipon* occurs in Phil 4:8 and is followed by fifteen additional verses on a completely new topic. Second, the present tense of the imperatives does not issue a new concern ("Beware of") but a concern of which Paul earlier apprised the Philippians: "*Continue* to look out for . . ." This makes "to write the same things to you is not burdensome" an introduction to what follows rather than a conclusion to what preceded in the letter. Third, paraenetic material commonly precedes the close of Paul's letters (e.g., Rom 12–15; Gal 5–6; Eph 4–6; Col 3–4; 1 Thess 4–5). So, its presence at this point in Philippians would be typical versus unusual.

Purpose in Writing

A call to rejoice despite their circumstances is Paul's first purpose in writing. The terms "rejoice" and "joy" are found fifteen times in Philippians' four chapters (1:4, 18, 25; 2:2, 17 (4x), 18, 28, 29; 3:1; 4:1, 4, 10). No other letter has these many occurrences. This is the theme of the letter. Paul did not accept financial support from any other church plant, indicating a close relationship with the Philippian church. This explains his "joy," when recalling their relationship. His affection for them is unlike that of any other church: "For God is my witness, how I long for all of you with the affection of Christ Jesus" (1:8).

A call for unity is Paul's second purpose. Paul gets news that the church was facing strong opposition from within and without. In Phil 1:27–28 Paul instructs the church: "Whether I come and see you or only hear about you in my absence, I will know that you stand firm in one spirit, contending as one person for the faith of the gospel, without being frightened in any

way by those who oppose you." The church at Philippi was facing two obstacles. First, their founder was in prison facing a trial with a life or death
verdict. Second, this made the opposition in Philippi "bold" and the church
was fearful of the same thing happening to them. Rather than claiming his
Roman citizenship rights, Paul allowed himself to be put in a Philippian
prison to protect the church from future attacks (see above). However, now
he was not able to do so. What he is able to do is to set before them the
model of Christ, who sacrificed himself for them and gained the victory
against his opponents through that sacrifice: "Be of the same mind, having
the same love, being in full accord and of one mind . . . with Christ as your
example" (2:2, 5).[21]

Paul's third purpose in writing has to do with internal division. The
church was divided about how to deal with external opposition. In particular there was a dispute between two key church leaders, Euodia and
Syntyche, that was affecting the church's ability to face outside opposition
with a united front (4:2–3): "I urge Euodia and I urge Syntyche to be of the
same mind in the Lord." He also asks an unnamed "loyal companion" to
"help these women, for they have struggled beside me in the work of the
gospel."[22]

Paul's fourth purpose is to inform the church about upcoming travel
plans: (1) He is sending Timothy (2:19–23). (2) He hopes to come himself
at some point (v. 24). (3) He is also sending Epaphroditus back to them
(2:25–30). Although Timothy was a member of the church-planting team,
Paul provides his credentials. He also commends Epaphroditus and explains
his delay. This may be an effort to address possible criticism. Perhaps there
was some criticism that Epaphroditus had not completed his appointed
task and was deserting Paul by returning to Philippi (2:25–30).[23] Providing
Timothy's credentials is probably a reminder of the help that he can provide
in light of internal and external opposition. Paul further anticipates his own
return to Philippi and announces a hopeful visit (2:23–24).

Paul's final purpose is to thank them for the gifts that the church sent
him via Epaphroditus. "I have been paid in full," Paul states, "and have
more than enough. I am fully satisfied, now that I have received from

---

21. Peterlin 1995.
22. See Culpepper 1980: 349–58; Dahl 1995: 3–15.
23. Buchanan 1964: 157–66.

Epaphroditus the gifts you sent, a fragrant offering, a sacrifice acceptable and pleasing to God" (4:10–20).[24]

Letter Structure

Philippians closely follows the structure of the first-century Hellenistic letter:[25]

> Letter Opening (1:1–2)
>> A (Sender) to B (Recipient),
>> Greeting/Health Wish
>
> Thanksgiving and Intercession (1:3–11): "I thank my God always . . ."
>> Thanksgiving (1:3–8)
>> Intercession (1:9–11)
>
> Body of the Letter
>> Body Opening (1:12–14)
>>> Disclosure: "I want you to know . . ."
>>
>> Body Middle (1:15—4:20) Advances the disclosure
>>> Paul's Imprisonment and Trial (1:15–30)
>>> A Call for Unity (2:1–18)
>>> Upcoming Visit (2:19—3:1)
>>>> Travel Plans:
>>>>> Timothy (vv. 19–23): "I hope to send Timothy to you . . ."
>>>>>
>>>>> Paul (v. 24): "I trust in the Lord that I will also come soon . . ."
>>>>>
>>>>> Epaphroditus (vv. 25–30): "I think it necessary to send to you Epaphroditus"
>>>>
>>>> Expressions Urging Responsible Action:
>>>>> "Welcome him in the Lord . . ." (v. 29)
>>>>> "Risking his life to make up for those services that you could not give me" (v. 30)
>>>>
>>>> Reference to Writing: "To write these things to you is not troublesome" (3:1a)
>>>
>>> Paraenesis (3:1b—4:9)
>>>> A Command to continue to be on the lookout for the dogs . . . (3:2–21)

---

24. See Hagelberg 2007; Peterman 1997.
25. Doty 1973: 34–35; White 1986: 198–211.

Body Closing
    A Request for Leadership Unity (4:1–3)
    A Call for Ethical Conduct (4:4–9)
    A Thank-you Note (4:10–20)
Letter Closing (4:21–23)
    Greetings to: "Greet all God's people in Christ Jesus "
    Greetings from: "All God's people greet you"
    Goodbye/Health Wish: "The grace of the Lord Jesus Christ be with your spirit"

Philippians 1

Letter Opening And Greeting (1:1–2)

> ¹From Paul and Timothy, Christ Jesus' servants, to all God's people
> in union with Christ Jesus together with the overseers and deacons
> who live in Philippi. ²Grace to you and peace from God our father
> and the Lord Jesus Christ.

Paul follows the standard letter-writing conventions of his day. Letters
back then opened with: "From A to B, Greetings." Everything beyond this
standard opening forecasts something about the sender's concerns and reasons for writing. In this letter opening, there are a number of additions (in
bold): From Paul **and Timothy Christ Jesus' servants** to **all God's people
in union with Christ Jesus together with the overseers and deacons** who
live in Philippi.

Paul often includes the name of a colleague. Here it is **Timothy**. However, while other letters continue in the "we" mode to reflect multiple send-
ers (e.g., 2 Corinthians, 1–2 Thessalonians), Philippians does not. The rest
of the letter is first person "I." Timothy would have been familiar with the
church as one of the church planters (Acts 16). So why is Timothy included?
The inclusion of a co-sender was common in letters where the co-sender
is the carrier or where there is a need for someone to verify the contents
of the letter. This is similar to a notary today. Epaphroditus (not Timothy) is identified as the letter carrier (2:25–30). Yet, Paul does plan to send
Timothy and he lists his credentials and noble character at unusual length
(2:19–24), suggesting a concern of some sort about Timothy's reception by
the church (see below). Throughout the letter Paul refers to strong opponents and expresses concern for the church's unity and steadfastness. Given

Paul's inability to visit them at this time, he may be simply be reminding the church of Timothy's partnership and that Paul is sending his very best.

What is noticeable in the letter's opening is the absence of "Paul an apostle of Christ Jesus by the will of God" that occurs in all but four of Paul's letters (Phil, 1–2 Thess, Phlm) and especially where his apostleship is in question (Rom, 1-2 Cor, Gal, Eph, Col, 1–2 Tim, Titus). Its absence here indicates a relationship of trust and confidence. In fact Paul uses strong language, when describing his feelings toward the church: "You are very dear to my heart" (1:9); "I long for all of you with the affection of Christ Jesus himself" (1:8). Instead, Paul identifies both he and Timothy as **Christ Jesus' servants**. The Greek word is *douloi* ("slaves"). It indicates that, although Paul is a Roman citizen and obligated to Rome, his ultimate obligation is to Christ.

The recipients are **all God's people in union with Christ Jesus**. Others translate the recipients as "saints" (Greek *hagioi*). The addition of **all** and **Christ Jesus** is noteworthy. In fact, **Christ Jesus** appears three times in this brief letter opening. Paul may well be anticipating his command in chapter 2 that **all** behave as Christ Jesus did in humbling himself and taking on the role of a servant. Also, this is the only letter in which Paul includes the leadership of **overseers and deacons** as recipients. It anticipates the overarching concern for a united strategy in facing opposition and a specific concern that **Euodia and Syntyche** (as part of the leadership team) agree (4:2).

The letter opening concludes with a greeting: **Grace to you and peace from God our father and the Lord Jesus Christ.** First-century letters simply used the Greek word "Greetings" (*chairein*). It was usually followed by "I pray that you are in good health" (*euchomai se hygiainein*). This is not unlike our: "Hope all is well with you and yours." Paul is quite intentional about how he phrases his greeting. **Grace** (*charis*) replaces the Greek *chairein* and the Hebrew wish for **peace** (*shalom*) is added. *Shalom* is a religious disposition that refers to inner rest and freedom from anxiety (Rom 15:13).[1] Then the source of grace and peace is identified as "**from God our father and the Lord Jesus Christ.**" Virtually every one of Paul's letters (with minor variations) opens this way. There is only one God, who became **God our father** through the death and resurrection of **the Lord Jesus Christ** (1:3).

---

1. See Werner Foerster, "εἰρήνη," *TDNT* 2:418. My own translation of Philippians precedes each section and is in bold in the rest of the text. Otherwise the NRSV is cited except where noted.

Thanksgiving and Intercession (1:3–11)

The Form

Four Hellenistic letter elements appear in the Paul's thanksgiving section:

- Thanks: "I thank my God" (1:3)

- Remembrance: "every time you come to mind" (1:3)

- Mention of faith/faithfulness: "because of your contribution to the gospel ministry" (1:5)

- Prayer for their spiritual progress: "I pray that . . ." (1:9)

One can tell how Paul feels about his reader(s) by what he includes and does not include of these four elements. When writing to a church where there is a good relationship, thanks, remembrance, faith, and prayer are found (e.g., Philippians; 1–2 Thessalonians; Philemon). Where the relationship is strained, remembrance, faith, and prayer are conspicuously absent (1 Corinthians) or a statement of thanks is missing entirely (e.g., 2 Corinthians; Galatians). In Philippians all four elements are present, indicating a good relationship between Paul and the church.

The Pauline thanksgiving section is longer than the typical first-century statement of thanks to a god or goddess for safe travel or good health. For example, a marine recruit named Apion thanks the god Serapis for delivering him from a storm at sea, while traveling to his military post (*BGU* 2.423). In part this is because Paul moves two elements which typically appear in the Hellenistic letter opening, namely, prayer and remembrance, to the thanksgiving section. In Paul's letters "I thank God" is followed by "when I remember you" and "because of your faith/faithfulness." Then he proceeds to pray for his readers: "I pray that . . ."

Paul's Thanksgiving for Participation in the Gospel Ministry (1:3–8)

> [3] I thank my God every time you come to mind. [4] And every time I pray for you, I make my petitions joyfully on your behalf [5] because of your contribution to the gospel ministry from the first day until now. [6] As a result I am confident that he who began a good work among you will complete it by the day Christ Jesus returns [7] It is right for me to think this way about you all because you are constantly in my thoughts, partnering with me in this ministerial privilege both when I am in prison as well as when I am out

> defending and confirming the gospel message. [8]God is my witness
> how I long for all of you with the affection of Christ Jesus himself.

For Paul and his readers, **thanks** is given to the one **God** versus the many gods and goddesses of the Greeks and Romans. Moreover, he thanks a personal and relational God. He is **my God. Every time you come to mind** (1:3) or remembrance of the recipient(s) was a standard part of the first-century letter. In *BGU 2.632* Apion (the same recruit) writes to his sister Sabina: "Before all things I pray that you are in health . . . Remembering you before the gods here." There was no separation of religion and state in antiquity. Every aspect of life was religious. There were household gods, business gods, guild gods, personal gods, and the cult of the emperor to which all imperial subjects were obliged. For Paul, however, it is thinking about the Philippian church that leads him to give thanks and to pray for them. There is nothing perfunctory or stereotypical about thanking God. Thoughts of the church evoke gratitude and joy. He remarks: **Every time I pray for you, I make my petitions joyfully on your behalf** (1:4). His "joy" is **because of your contribution to the gospel ministry from the first day until now** (1:5). Paul's uses the Greek word *koinōnia* to describe the Philippians' **contribution**. It is inaccurate to translate the term as "fellowship" and understand Paul to be referring to social interaction. *Koinōnia* has to do with acts of charity to meet financial and other physical needs (LSJ). Nor does *koinōnia* refer to socialism. The statement "the Jerusalem Church had all things in common" (*koina*; Acts 4:32) must be understood in context. It was when a need arose that someone in the church (such as Barnabas) sold a piece of property and gave the proceeds to the church (Acts 4:36–37).

Paul thanks the church later in the letter for the financial support that they sent by means of Epaphroditus (4:10–18). Their support was not only for Paul's physical needs but also to enable Paul to continue preaching **the gospel.** Nor was their support a one-time deal. **From the first day until now** indicates ongoing support from their founding (c. 50 AD) to the writing of this letter (c. 62 AD). Their support was also not that of a fair-weather friend. The church supported Paul, while he is now **in prison as well as when** he was **out defending and confirming the gospel message** (1:7).[2] This makes the Philippians co-workers **partnering with** Paul. Plus,

---

2. Gerald Hawthorne thinks that Paul's language of "defending" (*apologia*) the gospel message has to do with his trial in Rome (1983: xxxvi–xliv). However, *apologia is used* elsewhere of handling negative responses to his gospel message (Acts 22:1 "Hear the defense which I now make to you") or to himself (1 Cor 9:3: "my reply to those who sit in

their support was not merely that of writing a check or fulfilling a previ-ous pledge. Paul calls such support a **ministerial privilege.** Even more, the church did not give out of their abundance. They gave sacrificially. Three years earlier they "urgently pleaded" with Paul "for the privilege of sharing in this service to the people of God" in Jerusalem despite their desperate circumstances (2 Cor 8:4).

Paul's thanks involves more than financial support. His language is quite intimate: **Constantly in my thoughts** (1:7) and **how I long for all of you with the affection of Christ Jesus himself** (1:8) denote a beloved partner. No other church elicits this kind of language. **Constantly in my thoughts** is commonly translated "I have you in my heart" and **I long for all of you with the affection of Christ** is "I long for you with the bowels of Christ." Unlike anatomy today, Greek anatomy seated decision-making in the heart and emotions in the liver and intestines. According to Greek anatomy the viscera (*ta splanchna*) were the abdominal organs and were viewed as the origin of deeply felt emotions such as anger and love.[3] In English the term "heart" focuses primarily on one's emotions, whereas in Greek culture the emphasis was on the thinking that resulted in decisions (L&N), hence the translation **constantly in my thoughts**. The "bowels" (KJV; *ta splanchna*) in Greek anatomy, by contrast, were the seat of feelings and **affection** (LSJ). The closest we come to this today is the expression "a *gut* feeling." Elsewhere Paul uses *ta splanchna* of the affection he and Titus had for the Corinthian church (2 Cor 6:12; 7:15), affection as a fruit of the Spirit (Col 3:12), and of the fondness that believers should have for one another (Phlm 6, 12, 20). Here it is the deep feelings Paul has for the Philippian church.

Paul prefaces his statement of how deeply he feels about the Philippian church with the oath **God is my witness** (Phil 1:8). Why he needs to do so is debated. Paul's use of an oath is rare. Elsewhere, he uses the phrase to guarantee the truthfulness of what he is about to say (Rom 1:9; 2 Cor 1:23; 1 Thess 2:5, 10). Today we use such phrases as "with God as my witness" or "I swear to tell the truth." While our context is typically a court of law, for Paul it is the court of public opinion. It is where Paul's primary reason for writing is to confront an attempt to discredit his ministry or his care for the

judgment over me"). Paul's defense before the Jerusalem crowd (Acts 22:1), Festus (Acts 25:16), and Agrippa (Acts 26:1) are good examples.

3. Hawthorne states that *ta splanchna* did not include the intestines (1983: 25). How-ever, primary sources indicate otherwise. See LSJ 1996: s.v. and L&N 1988–1989: s.v.

church to whom he writes. Here as well, Paul likely took this solemn oath because he was aware that there were those who were not at all convinced of his right to lead them nor certain of the reality of his love for them. (See below.)

Paul's statement **as a result I am confident that he who began a good work among you will complete it by the day Christ Jesus returns** (1:6) in the midst of this language of intimacy seems a bit out of place. Expressions of confidence typically occur at the conclusion of the body of the letter as a means of urging responsible action. "I write to you confident of your obedience" (to his request; Phlm 21). Here, Paul's confidence is in God, who is credited as **he who began a good work** and **will complete** it. The **good work** is spiritual in nature and hence not a human accomplishment. It is something God initiated and something Paul is confident he will complete **by the day Christ Jesus returns.** This is not to say that believers aren't responsible for spiritual growth and maturity. It is a divine-human partnership. "By grace" we are "saved through faith" and "this is not" our "own doing; it is the gift of God" (Eph 2:8). Yet, we are what he has made us, namely, "created in Christ Jesus for good works" (Eph 2:10). Here also, the Philippians are at work **partnering with** [Paul] **in this ministerial privilege** and God is at work. The fact that Paul places this confidence right at the start of the letter signals a concern about the opposition within and without that the Philippian church is facing (see below). Doubts in the midst of persecutions are understandable. Doubts about Paul's concern for them (Epaphroditus' delay) and perhaps even God's concern for them may also be understandable. Both need correction and assurance.

Completion is anticipated **the day Christ Jesus returns.** "The Day of Christ" is shorthand for Christ's return which is often referred to as the *parousia* (Greek for "coming," "arrival"). The **Day** in both the Old Testament and the New Testament is a day of judgment. The Old Testament concept of the Day of the Lord is "darkness, not light, and gloom with no brightness in it" (Amos 5:20; cf. Joel 2:2). The day of the Lord in the New Testament is similarly a day of judgment. For unbelievers it is a "day of wrath" (1 Thess 5:9) that will come unexpectedly "as a thief comes in the night" (1 Thess 5:2). "When they [the world] say, 'There is peace and security,' then sudden destruction will come upon them, as labor pains come upon a pregnant woman, and there will be no escape!" (1 Thess 5:3). For believers it is the day when Christ comes to bring relief to the persecuted (2 Thess 1:6) and inflicts "vengeance on those who do not know God" and "do not obey the gospel of our Lord Jesus" (2 Thess 1:8). It is also a time when the church's leaders will be tested with fire (1 Cor 3:13) and when all believers will come before the judgment seat (*bēma*) of Christ (2 Cor 5:10).

Paul's Prayer For The Philippians' Growth in Knowledge and Insight (1:9–11)

> [9]I pray that your love will increase more and more in knowledge and depth of insight [10]so that you can discern what really matters and thereby remain sincere and faultless until the day Christ returns, [11]filled with the good fruit that comes through Jesus Christ and brings glory and praise to God

Paul's prayer for the Philippian church is fourfold:

- that their love will increase more and more in knowledge and depth of insight
- that they can discern what really matters
- that they remain sincere and faultless until the day Christ returns
- that they be filled with the good fruit that comes through Jesus Christ and brings glory and praise to God

Paul's prayer for "knowledge and insight," "discernment," "sincerity," and "good fruit" signals once again the major concern of the letter, namely, understanding how to face opposition and remain faultless in the process.

Paul acknowledges that the Philippians possess **love**. What he prays for is that their love **will increase more and more in knowledge and depth of insight.** Theologically, Paul is stating that love properly expressed depends on insightful knowledge. In Paul's writings **love** is a moral attribute involving self-sacrifice. By **knowledge,** he is not thinking of "head" knowledge. This is clear from the fact that knowledge is coupled with **insight** (*aisthēsei*). To have insight is to have the power of moral discrimination and ethical judgment.[4] It is to have a clear understanding that teaches Christian love how to make the best choices possible.

Paul expands on this in verses 10 to 11. **Knowledge and insight** result in the ability to **discern what really matters.** To **discern** (*dokimazein*) means to test and thereby have something's worth proven. In context this involves being able to recognize the things that have proven value (L&N).

---

4. Delling, "αἰσθήσει," *TDNT* 1:188.

In so doing, the church can remain **sincere and faultless.** Most modern translations render the Greek *eilikrineis* as "pure" and misunderstand Paul to be referring either to moral perfection or to sexual abstinence. Many church youth groups encourage their teens to fill out a purity pledge to abstain from sex before marriage. While that is noble, it is not what the Greek term means. In the culture of the day, it was used of having one's motives exposed by the sunlight and shown to be sincere ("pure motives"). The Greek *aposkopoi* is similarly translated "blameless" or "without blemish." However, the term means "to not cause stumbling." It is a person who takes care not to put anything in someone's way that would cause that person to trip and fall (L&N).

Sincerity and faultlessness in turn result in being **filled with the good fruit that comes through Jesus Christ and brings glory and praise to God.** Paul's imagery here is drawn from an orchard setting. The Philippians are now pictured as trees loaded down with a full crop (*peplērōmenoi*) of good fruit ready to be harvested. This "good fruit" (literally "righteous fruit) is the fruit that comes from right-living. It comes from acts of kindness and deeds of compassion toward each other and our neighbors. Paul makes it clear, however, that this crop of goodness is not self-generated. Nor can it be, for the **fruit** he has in mind is produced **through Jesus Christ** (*ton dia 'Iēsou*) and causes others to **praise God** because of it.

Fusing the Horizons: Thankfulness and Charity

Thankfulness for his churches and co-workers was part-and-parcel of the apostle Paul's daily routine. It is a quality that is in much demand as a new covenant people today. Whenever Paul thought about the Philippian church, thankfulness was his response. This was not just sometimes but always. It is rare, when we think of the church today, that our first response is thankfulness. This is especially the case in places where success, money, and possessions are the goal.

What is particularly remarkable is that Paul is thankful despite the tyrannical empire in which he lived and the opposition and suffering that he endured. This was also the situation of the Philippian church. Yet, Paul notes that, instead of hatred, bitterness and selfishness, love, joy, and generosity were hallmarks of this church. The Greek term *agapē* or "love" has to do with waiving self-interest in the interest of others. Love is not a matter of the heart ("my valentine") but of the will. It is a deep caring for others that arises from the work of God's Spirit within us. Christian love is not a feeling as most understand love today but a willingness to consider the needs of others ahead of our own needs and the personal sacrifice needed to meet those needs. In our "selfie"-oriented culture, love as self-sacrifice is a much-needed virtue.

The Philippian church expressed their love through concrete acts of generosity.[5] The Greek term *koinōnia* is unhelpfully translated "fellowship" today and thought of in terms of social interaction. However, the Greek term has more to do with acts of charity to meet the physical needs of the body of Christ. A charitable heart is the work of God's Spirit and a mark of Christian maturity. This was evident in the Philippian church. Despite their severe financial straits, they not only gave to others but begged for the opportunity to help other churches who were in need (2 Cor 8:2). "I can testify," Paul states, "that they voluntarily gave . . . beyond their means, begging us earnestly" (2 Cor 8:3–5). What motivated the church to give sacrificially? Paul says that they gave themselves first to the Lord. "Seek the kingdom of God above all else and live righteously," Jesus tells his disciples, "and he will give you everything that you need" (Matt 6:33 NLT). They also saw giving to others as a ministerial privilege ("begging us earnestly for the privilege of sharing in this ministry," 2 Cor 8:4).

"Joy" is the theme of Paul's letter. It is referenced more times in this short letter than in the rest of Paul's letters combined (1:4, 18, 25; 2:2, 17 [4x], 18, 28, 29; 3:1 4:1, 4). Despite our circumstances, the joy of the Lord is our strength. The Philippians had this in spades. It was their "abundant joy" that led the church to overflow in "a wealth of generosity on their part" (2 Cor 8:2). They understood that the joy of the Lord was their strength (Neh 8:10).

The Philippians' sacrificial giving and view of ministry as a partnership are models for us today. Giving is all too often thought of as a church requirement and a fixed percentage. Finances is one of the top leading causes of both marital and church breakups. Fractured relationships between spouses and church members would diminish, if we viewed giving as a divine partnership and as a ministerial privilege. Too often the relational dysfunction of the world is found in our churches instead of the Spirit-inspired love, joy, goodness, generosity, and faithfulness that epitomized the Philippian church. The ultimate example is found in Jesus, who provides us with an example of the ultimate

5. See Belleville 1996: 211–12.

sacrifice, first in humbling himself by taking on human form (Phil 2:7) and second, by dying on a cross in our place (Phil 2:8).

PAUL'S SITUATION:

The Gospel Advances Despite Imprisonment And Opposition (1:12–18)

> [12] I want you to know, brothers and sisters that everything that has happened to me has served to advance the gospel rather than hinder it. [13]As a result it has become clear throughout the Imperial guard and to all the rest that my imprisonment is because I preach Christ. [14]Consequently the majority of brothers and sisters in the Lord have been emboldened by my imprisonment to fearlessly dare to speak out more and more. [15]Some who proclaim Christ do it out of envy and rivalry, but others do it out of goodwill. [16]The latter do so out of love, since they know that I have been placed here to defend the gospel. [17]The former who proclaim Christ do it for selfish rather than pure reasons, thinking to cause me harm while I am in prison. [18]Yet, what does it matter except that Christ is proclaimed in any way possible, whether the motivation is genuine or not. For this reason I rejoice and will continue to rejoice. [19]For I know that through your intercession to God and through the help of Jesus Christ's Spirit this will result in my deliverance. [20]It remains my eager expectation and hope that I will not be ashamed in any way but that Christ will now as always be magnified in my body by my bold proclamation, whether through life or through death

The church at Philippi faced two obstacles. First, their leader was in prison and facing a Roman trial. This made the opposition against the church bold: "Where is your fearless leader now?" "Look what happens to those who follow Christ!" This also made the church fearful of the same thing happening to them. Second, the church was divided about what to do. There were strong, opinionated people in the church (2:5). In particular, there was a dispute between two key church leaders, Euodia and Syntyche, that was affecting the church's ability to face outside opposition with a united front (4:2–3). To make matters worse, there were Christian preachers that were causing problems for Paul: **Some who proclaim Christ do it out of envy and rivalry . . . thinking to cause me harm while I am in prison** (1:15–17).

Paul's strategy is to encourage the church by providing good news. He introduces this information with the stereotypical language of his day: "I want you to know." Here (per the letters of his day) it introduces Paul's primary reason for writing. Virtually all of Paul's letters fall into the category of either a request ("I ask you [*parakalō*]. . ."; 1 Cor 1:10, 2 Thess 2:1; Phlm 9),[6] disclosure (" I want you to know [*ginōskein*]"); Rom 1:13, 2 Cor 1:8, Phil 1:12, Col 2:1) or a reminder of what had already been disclosed ("You know"; 1 Thess 2:1). Another type of letter is that of rebuke ("I am amazed . . ."). Galatians is Paul's only letter of rebuke ("I am astonished that you are so quickly deserting . . ."; 1:6). Letters of compliance ("In accordance with your instructions, I have . . ."), hearing ("I heard that . . ."), and relief ("I rejoiced when I heard that you are well") are also common reasons for writing in Paul's day.

Paul's strategy also includes reminding the Philippians that they are family, **brothers and sisters.** This is a typical reminder for all Paul's churches. They are in this together as family members should be. Although many modern translations render *adelphoi* as "brothers," it is clear from the context that Paul is addressing the entire congregation. "Brothers and sisters" (NET, NRSV, NLT), "dear friends" (NEB), and "my friends" (REB) are more accurate renderings. Paul's language is not patriarchal, including only men as family members. The women are equally partners in advancing the gospel. In fact, the church met in a woman's house (Lydia; Acts 16) and two women were leaders of the Philippian church (Phil 4:2–3).

The good news that Paul has to pass along is that the gospel has not been jeopardized by his imprisonment. In fact, it has helped to further **advance the gospel. To advance** translates a Greek term that means to move forward in spite of an obstruction or stumbling block (*prokoptēn*). It is used of removing the danger that would block the traveler's path (LSJ). The tense is perfect: "in a state of advancing the gospel." The progress of the gospel was so great that it had **become clear throughout the imperial guard and**

---

6. *Parakalō* and *deomai* are commonly mistranslated "I beg you," "I appeal to you," "I beseech you," or "I exhort you." Given our knowledge of the Greek letter, *parakalō* and *deomai* are stereotypical terms of request—"I ask you" or "I urge you." *Parakalō* is typically used by one who has the authority to command but waives this right and *deomai* is a request between equals. The language of "beseech" or "beg" is used, when addressing dignitaries. For a detailed analysis of the formulaic features of the Hellenistic letter, see White 1971: 93.

to all the rest that my imprisonment is because I preach Christ (v. 13). **Imperial** translates the Greek *praitōrion*. The Praetorian guard was an elite unit of the Roman army, whose members served as personal bodyguards to the Roman emperors. Some claim that the Praetorians also served as bodyguards for high-ranking officials such as senators or provincial governors. However, this was only during the era of the Roman Republic. With the Republic's transition into the Roman Empire, the Praetorians became the Emperor's personal security detail.[7] **And to all the rest** probably refers to **those of Caesar's household** (4:22). The average Roman household included more than immediate family members. Similar to the aristocratic estates of Europe, the household included extended family, business partners, staff, and frequent visitors. It took a large staff to run a household. Both freemen and slaves were entrusted with a wide range of positions and responsibilities. The Imperial household was enormous, and the offices and duties were minutely divided and subdivided.[8]

The advance of the gospel message and news that Paul's imprisonment was **because I preach Christ** resulted in **the majority of** Philippian **brothers and sisters in the Lord** to **become emboldened** (v. 14). **Emboldened** translates a perfect tense. The majority are not just momentarily encouraged but in a confident state of mind (*pepoithotas*). The **majority** of brothers and sisters suggests there was a Christian minority that was not supportive of Paul. Paul's language **fearlessly dare to speak out more and more** suggests strong opposition. One group supports Paul **out of love** and **goodwill.** They know that Paul is in prison **to defend the gospel** (v. 16). The other group proclaims Christ **out of envy and rivalry** (v. 15). **Envy** suggests that this group is driven by jealousy of Paul's success as an evangelist. **Rivalry** is sometimes translated "strife." However, the type of strife referred to by the Greek term *eris* is frequently verbal, for example, saying bad things about one another or never having a good word to say (L&N). Their reasons are **selfish** (*phthonos*) denoting a state of ill will toward someone because of some real or presumed advantage (LSJ). They did not preach Christ for **pure reasons** and they were motivated by self-interest (*eritheia*), wanting to be better than someone else or wanting to make people think they are better (L&N; v. 17). They present a public face of sincerity, but inwardly they are driven by greed.

---

7. See Cowan 2014 and de la Bedoyere 2017.
8. See Lanciani 1890: 106–34.

Their goal may have been to divert Paul's base of ministerial support to themselves. The Philippian church was Paul's only supporting church. It was the only one from which he would accept financial support: "Look! Paul's out of the picture. *Carpe diem.* Seize the day!" They had a good cover story. They **proclaim Christ**. However, they did it in a way to stir up trouble for Paul **thinking to cause me harm while I am in prison** (v. 17). Evangelism was their cover and the Bible was their tool. Similar to Job's so-called three friends (Job 4–23), Paul's opponents likely claimed that his arrest was a sign of God's judgment of wrong-doing (v. 15)., However, Paul picks a very specific Greek term (*thlipsis*) to describe what he was experiencing. In the New Testament *thlipsis* denotes suffering for the sake of Christ and not suffering due to sinful actions (BDAG). Paul also says, **I have been placed here** (v. 16) The Greek *keimai* is a divine passive, indicating that God is in control (Anlex).

Paul's attitude toward his opponents is noteworthy. He was magnanimous: **What does it matter except that Christ is proclaimed in any way possible, whether the motivation is genuine or not. For this reason I rejoice and I will continue to rejoice** (v. 18). Paul was not always so magnanimous. Toward some from the Jerusalem church, who wanted to make a good impression outwardly by compelling the Gentiles in Galatia to be circumcised (Gal 6:12), Paul says: "As for those agitators, I wish they would go the whole way and castrate themselves!" (Gal 5:12). Paul said this in c. 47 AD. Now fifteen years later facing a Roman trial for preaching Christ, Paul was able to be magnanimous. Magnanimous is defined as "courageously noble in mind and heart; generous in forgiving; eschewing resentment or revenge; unselfish."[9] How he managed this was through the church's prayers on his behalf: **I know that through your intercession to God and the help of Jesus Christ's Spirit this will result in my deliverance** (v. 19).

The combination of human responsibility and divine help are key in Paul's theology. Human responsibility comes in the form of *deēseōs* or intercessions to God on Paul's behalf. There is no such thing as a lone Christian. **Help** from Christ's Spirit is the term *epichorēgias*. The Spirit makes available whatever is necessary to help or supply the needs of someone (L&N). The picture is of the human body, where Christ is the head from whom the whole body's ligaments and sinews are supported and held together by Christ's Spirit (Col 2:19; cf. Eph 4:16). Given both human and divine support, Paul states that this will **result in** his **deliverance. Deliverance** is the

---

9. Gove 1993: s.v. Definition from *Webster's Dictionary.*

Greek word *sōtērian*. Though commonly translated "salvation," here it likely has to do with a court verdict. This is clear from Paul's outlook of **eager expection** and **hope** (one article + two nouns; Granville Sharp's rule).[10] **Eager expectation** pictures Paul craning his neck to catch a glimpse of what is ahead. **Christ will now as always be magnified in my body by my bold proclamation whether through life or through death** (v. 20). **In my body** is perhaps better understood as by his life. Paul has in mind his total life as a responsible human being and Christ's servant. The term **magnify** recognizes the importance of someone by paying great respect to that person and to highly honor (LSJ). To **magnify Christ** is to cause people to respond in praise of Christ by how Paul lives. There is no hint that Paul's response to his situation was that of embarrassment. **I will not be ashamed in any way.** Also he had a martyr's mentality. There is no hint that he was driven by fear to renounce Christ. Instead he continued not only to **proclaim Christ** but to do so **boldly. Whether through life or through death** is not Paul considering the possibility of execution.[11] He is simply asserting that, even after he dies, there will not be a basis for faulting his ministry or accusing him of misconduct.

Fusing the Horizons: Being Christ in Today's World

What about our pastors and evangelists? What would be our response to their imprisonment for preaching the gospel? Some undoubtedly would say that our pastor must have committed a crime to warrant imprisonment. Even worse would be hearing that our pastor was arrested for an alleged act of terrorism or sexual assault. It is times like these that bring out the best and the worst in people. There are always those inside and outside the church who are eager and waiting to exploit bad news or even to create it. We call these people "gossips" or "rumormongers." This sin, in my opinion, is particularly deadly: "Rumors are dainty morsels that sink deep into one's heart" (Prov 18:8 NLT). They have destroyed more people, stained more reputations, broken more friendships and split more churches than any other sin I've experienced.

10. Granville Sharp's Rule: "When the conjunction *kai* connects two nouns (or equivalents) preceded by a single article, the latter always relates to the same person that is expressed or described by the first noun or participle" (Sharp 1803: 3). In English compare: "We met with **the** owner and operator of the establishment."

11. Roman citizens like Paul were executed with a sword, which, unlike crucifixion, was considered an honorable death. See "Beheading" *EB* 2008.

Rumors are swiftly told, quickly heard, rapidly spread, and, worst of all, are readily believed.

Because we tend to use information (true or false) as a tool in building relationships and partnerships, gossip gets woven into the fabric of most communities. It is a cancer that ultimately eats away at the core of a community's unity and trust until there is nothing left. What makes gossip particularly heinous is our attitude about it. Our society expects people to gossip, jokes about it, and spreads it.

The sin of gossiping needs to be confronted but rarely (if ever) is. Gossip in the church is a killer, especially when church staff are involved. At one church that our family attended, two church leaders engaged in gossip. Both left after considerable damage to the relational fabric of the congregation resulted.

Our job as Christians is to be Christ to those around us. It is not just a job for individual believers or even for the experts. The fact that we are to do it as "one" (as a local body of believers) makes the job even more daunting. There is no room for gossip or tale-telling, if the church is to succeed. Paul's description of this job is **contending** (*synathleō* 1:27). It is an athletic term for hand–to-hand combat. It is a picture of extreme exertion and intense discipline (L&N). The first Rocky Balboa movie is a good example.[12] It depicts Rocky running a bit farther each day and ascending more and more of the seventy-two steps that comprise the entrance to the Philadelphia Museum of Art.

Those of us in prominent roles in our local church should not be surprised by the extent to which others will go to undermine us. After all, our adversary, the Devil, prowls around like a roaring lion, looking for someone to devour (1 Pet 5:8). Our world like Paul's is driven by a jealousy of the success of others and by rivalry. There are those with an envious spirit or sheer selfish ambition, who are eager to undercut us.

---

12. *Rocky* (1976), dir. John G. Avildsen.

Paul's Perspective: To Live Is Christ. To Die Is Gain. (1:21–30)

[21]So for me to live is to continue preaching Christ and to die is gain. [22]Now, if I continue in this mortal body, this means fruitful work for me. What I will choose? I do not know. [23]I am pulled in two directions. I desire to depart and be with Christ, for that is far better for me. [24] Yet to remain is indispensible for you. [25]Because I am convinced of the latter, I know that I will remain and continue with all of you for the joyful progress of your faith. [26]Your boasting in Christ Jesus will then overflow on account of my returning to you. [27]Until then, live as citizens who are worthy of the good news about Christ so that whether I come and see you in person or whether I hear about you at a distance, I will know that you are standing firm in one spirit, striving side–by-side as one person for the gospel faith [28]and not terrified in any way by your opponents. This is evidence of their destruction but of your salvation. This is God's doing. [29]For he has granted you the privilege not only to believe in Christ but also to suffer for him, [30]You have the same sort of struggle you saw me face and now hear that I am facing again.

Paul has been under house arrest for two years and is now facing a Roman trial that has life and death implications. After months of reflecting on his situation, his conclusion is that life is gain but death is a greater gain. Although the Greek is often translated "For me to live is Christ and to die is gain," this literal translation does not capture Paul's meaning. We know this because "Christ" and "gain" are advantages. Yet commentators often personalize *Christos* and claim that "to live" is to have "Christ" (the person). The broader context indicates the opposite. Death is a **gain** because it means to be face-to-face with Christ. Paul states in Phil 1:23: **I desire to depart and be with Christ. To depart** (*analysai*) is a nautical term that means to "lift the anchor" so that the boat is free to navigate towards its heavenly destination (LSJ). "To live is Christ" is explained in verse 22: **If I continue in this mortal body, this means fruitful work for me,** that is, preaching the gospel. "To live is Christ" is thus Paul's shorthand for "To live is to preach the good news about Christ." A more accurate translation would therefore be: **For me to live is to continue preaching Christ.** Paul is **pulled in two directions:** To stay and continue preaching the gospel or to depart this life and be with his Lord and Savior, which is **far better for** him. The Greek is "torn between the two," similar to a game of tug-of-war that children play today. For Paul it is a tug of war between ministerial duty and personal desire. Paul's personal desire is **to depart and be with Christ**. The Greek word *epithymian* carries the sense of a longing or yearning (LSJ). For Paul (as for all believers) death is a homecoming: "Yes, we would rather be away from the body and at home with the Lord" (2 Cor 5:8). We have a variety of euphemisms for death: "He kicked the bucket," "she is pushing up flowers," or "they croaked." However, the Christian's response to death should be different: "He has gone to be with the Lord" and "She has passed into the presence of Christ" are more accurate.

To die was Paul's personal choice, his passion as it were. Death would allow his human boat to raise anchor and depart for the Christian home-land.[13] God's choice is another matter and Paul thinks that God's choice at this point in time is to **remain and continue with all of** them. There is more ministry to be accomplished. Paul's conviction is that it is not just necessary that he do so but **indispensable** (*anankaioteron* is a comparative; v. 24).

He concludes with the theme of "joy": **I know that I will remain and continue with all of you for the joyful progress of your faith** (v. 25). His **returning to** the Philippian church is indispensable. Their fear will change to **joy,** their faith will not stand still but **progress,** and their anxiety about the impact of confessing Christ in public will change to **boasting in Christ Jesus** (v. 26). In the meantime, Paul instructs the church to **live as citizens who are worthy of the good news about Christ** (v. 27). Roman citizenship was a privilege highly coveted in Paul's day by non-Romans. Some gained it through military service. Others bought citizenship. The Roman tribune in Jerusalem told Paul: "It cost me a large sum of money to get my citizen-ship" (Acts 22:28). Still others inherited it. Paul responded: "I was born a citizen" (v. 28). The fact that the Judean governor kept Paul in custody for two years, hoping for a bribe, indicates that Paul's family had enough wealth to procure citizenship (Acts 24:26). Citizens were afforded a range of rights, including due process (the right to sue, be sued, stand trial, appeal a verdict, be protected from imprisonment), property ownership, voting, making contracts, marriage, and self-governance.[14] For the Christian, how-ever, earthly citizenship was trumped by heavenly citizenship. As a citizen of God's "empire," the church's job is to **live** as someone **worthy of the good news about Christ.** This means "to conduct oneself with proper reference

13. See Droge 1988: 263–86 regarding ancient theories of suicide. See also Croy 2003: 517–31 about whether Paul was contemplating suicide.

14. "Roman Citizenship" *EB* 2008; Brewer 1954: 76–83.

to one's obligations in relationship to others and as part of a community" (L&N; Aristotle, *Pol.* A 1252a).

This was no easy task for the church, since they faced strong opponents (v. 28). How strong is indicated by Paul's use of the term **terrified** (*ptyromenoi*). Step one is unity. They need to be united spiritually, **standing firm in one spirit.** They also need to be united personally, **striving side-by-side as one person** (v. 27). Step two is theological perspective. Suffering for Christ is **evidence of their** opponents' **destruction** but of the church's **salvation** (v. 28). A similar idea is found in 2 Cor 2:15–16, where Paul states: "For we are the aroma of Christ to God among those who are being saved and among those who are perishing. To the one it is a fragrance from death to death. To the other it is a fragrance from life to life." It is God who is in control. **This is God's doing.** "God will repay with affliction those who afflict you and give relief to the afflicted as well as to us, when the Lord Jesus is revealed from heaven with his mighty angels in flaming fire, inflicting vengeance on those who do not know God and on those who do not obey the gospel of our Lord Jesus. They will suffer the punishment of eternal destruction, separated from the presence of the Lord and from the glory of his might" (2 Thess 1:7–9). Step three is also theological. **For he has granted** them **the privilege not only to believe in Christ but also to suffer for him** as well (v. 29). The Philippians are facing **the same struggle that** they **saw** Paul face **and now hear that** he is **facing again** (v. 30). The Greek term for **struggle** (*agona*) is graphic. An *agona* was an athletic contest that required the exertion and self-denial needed to face one's opponent (Anlex). The term for **suffer** is not Paul's usual term *thlipsis* (suffering as a Christian) but *paschein* ("to undergo an experience with the implication of physical or psychological suffering" (L&N). Paul calls suffering for Christ a **privilege.** As with Roman citizenship, heavenly citizenship has its responsibilities and its privileges. Paul views suffering not merely as a reality but as a privilege.

Fusing the Horizons: Dealing With Adversity

As Paul awaits trial, he considers the two possible outcomes. One is life and the other is death. Of the two, which is preferable? Although we might claim "no contest" for anything but life, Paul himself was torn between what was best for him and what was best for the church.

Paul's preference was death. Most of us probably find this difficult to understand but there is an important spiritual truth here. Paul desired death because then he would be face–to-face with the Lord Jesus Christ. Death is the way to go home. For the person who has accepted Christ as Savior and Lord and lives to serve Christ and him alone, death is a homecoming.

Paul teaches the same truth in 2 Cor 5:6–8: "Therefore we are always confident and know that, as long as we are at home in the body, we are away from the Lord . . . and would prefer to be away from the body and at home with the Lord." "At home with the Lord" is what happens to every believer at death. This is not a way to soften the reality of death. It is reality itself.

Yet, Paul chooses life, which is choosing to continue sharing the good news about Jesus Christ. Even so, sharing Christ in our society can become a fearful thing. Strong opposition evokes fear and fear takes us away from what we are called to be and to do as followers of Christ. However, we must be clear about what it means to be Christ to those around us. For many, their only knowledge of Christ will come through watching what we do and listening to what we say. This means that everything we do and everything we say must be what Christ would do and what Christ would say. Jesus used the metaphors of "salt" and "light" to get this across to his disciples. Like salt, we must seek to preserve what is right and true in a decaying world (Matt 5:13). We must also be light to those around us. One might think that evangelism and witnessing is the job of professionals such as pastors and church leaders. Not so. Being Christ to those around us is the job of every believer, and it is the job of every local church. It is so much a part of our job that we are to do it as "one." We are to contend as one person for the truth of the gospel and not become discouraged by naysayers or cynics. Christians are commonly viewed as hypocrites today. In some cases, this is justifiable. However, we live in a world that does not tolerate those who claim that there is only "one way." To say that Christ alone is the way, the truth, and the life is increasingly viewed as "hate language," spoken by misanthropic people and the politically incorrect.

Being Christ to others has become a confusing and fearful task. People seem to hate each other more than ever. Protesters increasingly resort to mob violence and seek to intimidate and drown out any possibility of reasonable conversation. Incivility and name-calling have become the norm and we are categorized as either evil or good. Being Christ to such a broken society as ours should be our priority. Jesus was spit on, reviled, and mocked. We should expect no less and be prepared for it. The best response is not to respond in-kind (although we might feel like doing so) but to pray for those who persecute us. Again, Jesus said that it is easy to pray for our friends. It is much harder to pray for those who oppose us. This does not mean that we shrink from speaking truthfully. That is not an option. It is how we respond to those who do not accept it that is key.

Philippians 2

The Proper Frame of Mind: The Humility of Christ (2:1–11)

> [2:1]Therefore, if there is any encouragement from union with Christ, if any comfort from love, if any charity from spiritual unity, and if any tender compassion, [2]make my joy complete by having the same mind and the same love, and of being of one spirit and one accord. [3]Do nothing out of selfish ambition or groundless pride, but regard others with pride and yourselves with humility [4]Do not be fixated on yourselves but think about others. [5]Have this mind-set among you that was also in Christ Jesus.
> [6]Who, though prior to the incarnation, he existed in divine form,
>   he did not regard equal status with God as something to be grasped after.
> [7]Instead he emptied himself
>   by taking on the form of a servant and being born in the likeness of human beings.
> And after he found himself in the form of a human being,
>   [8]he humbled himself by becoming obedient to death even death by crucifixion.
> [9]Therefore God elevated him to the place of highest honor
>   and gave him the name above every other name
> [10]That at the name of Jesus
>   each and every knee will bow in heaven, on earth and under the earth.
> [11]And every tongue will publicly acknowledge
>   that Jesus Christ is Lord to the glory of God the Father.

This section does not introduce a new thought. It is linked to what precedes by the conjunction **therefore** (*oun*). Up to this point Paul has been concerned to fortify the church in its struggle against outside opponents. Now he turns his attention to the problem of congregational division that leaves the Philippians vulnerable to enemy attacks. The solution is summed up by the word "unite." Harmony is essential for the church to deal with outside opponents. They are to have the **same** mind, the **same** love, the **same** spirit and of **one** accord. Paul is not saying that they must all be mental robots. However, as a congregation facing opposition, they need to unite behind the same game plan in dealing with it.[1]

Paul issues two commands:

- Make my joy complete by having the same mind, love, spirit, and accord (v. 2)

- Have the same mindset that Christ Jesus had (v. 5)

He grounds these two commands in three conditional clauses that spell out what unites them: **Encouragement** from their union with Christ, **comfort** from the love that binds, **charity from spiritual unity** and **tender compassion**. The poetic and rhetorical character of these conditionals makes it difficult to translate with precision.[2]

The first term *paraklēsis* can refer to a summons, an exhortation, an encouragement, or an entreaty (LSJ). Here **encouragement** is perhaps the best fit. This encouragement is *en Christō*. The Greek preposition *en* is quite versatile. Location "in" is very common. However, there is a more dynamic component. It is encouragement that comes from their **union with Christ**, namely, from their living "in the sphere of Christ."[3] The second term *paramythion* is a synonym of *paraklēsis*. It can refer to encouragement, exhortation, comfort, or relief (LSJ). Following **encouragement**, **comfort** fits well. The genitive *agapēs* (**love**) is likely the source of their comfort.[4] The

1. Black 1985: 299–308.

2. For other examples of *ei* used in this way, see BDF 1961: 372.1.

3. Translations widely differ. Cf. NIV "If you have any encouragement from being united with Christ, if any comfort from his love, if any fellowship with the Spirit, if any tenderness and compassion"; NJB "So if in Christ there is anything that will move you, any incentive in love, any fellowship in the Spirit, any warmth or sympathy"; NLT "Is there any encouragement from belonging to Christ? Any comfort from his love? Any fellowship together in the Spirit? Are your hearts tender and compassionate?" NRSV "If then there is any encouragement in Christ, any consolation from love, any sharing in the Spirit, any compassion and sympathy."

4. Although, see G. Stählin, "παραμύθιον" *TDNT* 5:821, who thinks Paul is referring to his own love for the Philippians.

third term *koinōnia*, though commonly translated "fellowship," is a word that refers to financial participation (Anlex). The difficulty is how to understand *pneumatos* (literally, "the participation of the spirit"). Some think Paul has in mind **charity** that God's Spirit engenders.[5] It could also be the charity that springs from their **spiritual unity**.[6] The emphasis in this section on oneness and unity points to the latter construal. The final terms that describe their unity are "deep affection" (*splanchna*) and "tenderness" (*oiktirmoi*). *Splanchna* is an anatomical word for the intestines or "inner parts of the abdomen," which were considered the seat of the feelings and affections in Paul's day. Paul used the term earlier of the tender affection that he felt for the Philippians (1:8). *Oiktirmoi* is commonly used by Paul of God's mercy and compassion towards us. The word order of *tis* + two nouns connected by *kai* suggests a close linking of the two nouns with perhaps the meaning **tender compassion** (L&N).[7] The encouragement, comfort, charity, and tender compassion that God's people in Christ experience should produce oneness of **mind, love, spirit,** and **accord** (2:2). Paul's language is reminiscent of the command to love the Lord with all one's heart, mind, and strength (Mark 12:33; cf. Deut 6:5). Paul adds s**pirit**, which reflects the outpouring of the Spirit at Pentecost (Acts 2) and the enlivening of our spirit at conversion (Gal 4:6).

What follows are the "do-nots."

- Do nothing from selfish ambition or conceit, but in humility regard others as better than yourselves (v. 3 NRSV)

- Let each of you look not to your own interests, but to the interests of others (v. 4 NRSV)

Although most English translations like the NRSV have imperatives "Do nothing," "Regard others" and "Let each look not to," the Greek of verses 3 and 4 does not have any verbs. The main command is "Make my joy complete by being of the same mind, love, spirit, and accord" (v. 2). Verses 3 and 4 spell out how not to be. "Make my joy complete by NOT being . . ." They

---

5. However, see Hawthorne 1983: 66, who argues that 2 Cor 13:14 *he koinōnia tou hagiou pneumatos* ("the fellowship of the Holy Spirit") is a parallel so unusually close to the expression found in Phil 2:1 that one is fairly forced to admit that *pneumatos* can only refer to the Holy Spirit.

6. For "spiritual unity" the genitive *pneumatos* would be a genitive of the source of their charity.

7. An article or *ei tis* followed by two nouns connected by *kai* expresses a single idea ("tender compassion") rather than two separate ones. See BDF 1961: 276.

are not to have **selfish ambition**[8] or **groundless pride.** Selfish ambition is self-seeking rather than other-seeking. To be self-seeking is to be **fixated on** themselves and **their own interests** (*hekastos skopountes*). **Groundless pride** is pride that has no basis or justification. Instead of self-pride, they should rather have other-pride. This is pride in others and a healthy regard of self with humility. Some go too far and translate "but in humility regard others as better than yourselves" (NRSV). *Hyperechontas heauton* need only be a corrective of degree. Rather than elevate oneself, there is a need to view oneself with humility and to elevate others. In short, Paul is saying that they need to take pride in others and stop focusing only on themselves. Verse 4 also needs a bit of correction. "Not looking to one's own interests but to the interests of others" (v. 4) is not that black and white. Some insert "only" and "also" into the translation: "Look not ONLY to your own interests but ALSO to the interests of others." The Greek *hekastos skopountes* has to do with a total fixation on oneself to the exclusion of others. The sense then is to stop focusing inward and start looking outward. There can be no corporate unity, if some focus solely on themselves as being right and ignore what others think.

Christ is invoked as the exemplary model: **Have this mindset** as a church body **that was also in Christ Jesus.** The pronoun is plural (**among you**). The command is for a corporate oneness of mind (v. 5). The verses that follow are hymnic in character, raising the question of whether Paul was using a pre-existing hymn of the early church or employing a poetic composition of his own.[9] Scholarly literature abounds on this topic.[10] Signs of poetic style are the following. There is a shift stylistically from the narrative style of a first-century letter to that of a poetic, polished hymn. The relative pronoun *hos* is typical of a religious hymn as are the participles (*hyparchōn, labōn, genomenos, heuretheis, genomenos*).[11] The truths of salvation history point to a creedal formulation. However, verses 9 to 11 about

8. Some understand *eritheian* to refer to a feeling of resentfulness based upon jealousy and implying rivalry (L&N). Paul already has used *eritheia* in 1:17. There as here it carries overtones of a party-spirit generated by selfish ambition. "Rivalry" is guaranteed to destroy unity. Therefore, it must be eliminated. Compare F. Büchsel, "ἐριθεία," *TDNT* 2:660–61.

9. Johannes Weiss in 1899 was the first to notice the poetic, rhythmic nature of these verses. See Hawthorne 1983: 76 and Eckman 1980: 258–66. Compare Jeremias 1963, Lohmeyer 1976, and Martin 1997.

10. See the excursus below.

11. Versnel 1998: 209.

Christ's exaltation and the appropriateness of bowing the knee in worship are not immediately relevant to dealing with persecution and opposition. This suggests that Paul was inserting a preexisting piece that he kept intact.[12] The poetic structure is lost in most English translations.

> [6]Who, though prior to the incarnation, he existed in divine form,
>> he did not regard equal status with God as something to be grasped after
> [7]Instead he emptied himself
>> by taking on the form of a servant and being born in the likeness of human beings.
> And after he found himself in the form of a human being
>> [8]he humbled himself by becoming obedient to death, even death by crucifixion.
> [9]Therefore God elevated him to the place of highest honor
>> and gave him the name above every other name
> [10]That at the name of Jesus
>> each and every knee will bow in heaven, on earth and under the earth
> [11]And every tongue will publicly acknowledge
>> that Jesus Christ is Lord to the glory of God the Father

The central themes of self-sacrifice and humility found in verses 6 to 8 are exactly the model that the Philippian church needed to adopt. However, the condensed character of poetry makes unpacking the strophes a difficult exegetical and theological task. Grammatically the Christ-hymn starts with the relative pronoun *hos* ("who"), which recalls how other hymn-like confessions in the New Testament begin (cf. Col 1:15; 1 Tim 3:16; Heb 1:3). Even more importantly, *hos* ("who") links the hymn with what precedes: **Have this mindset among you that was also in Christ Jesus** (v. 5).

Theologically, Christ's divine existence preceded his human incarnation. Verse 6 assumes Christ's preexistence.[13] Christ's preexistence was **in the form** (*morphē*) **of God**. Some equate **form** with essence (*ousia*). He possessed the essence of deity. Others equate **form** with nature (*physis*). He shared the essential attributes of deity. Still others equate form with image. He was the visible manifestation of God. Yet, one need not have to choose. Both essence and attribute could be intended. Visible manifestation, however, was post-incarnation.

12. Ralph Martin devoted significant scholarly attention to Phil 2:6–11. See the bibliography for his extensive works.

13. Hawthorne 1983: 81.

Although prior to the incarnation, he possessed the essence and attributes of deity, the hymn goes on to declare that he did not regard **equal status with God something to be grasped after**. The Greek term *harpagmon* ("grasped after") is used of something done suddenly and powerfully. "Forcefully seize" is the sense. The Greek *isa theō* is commonly translated **equality with God**. This begs the question: What kind of equality with God did he not try to forcefully seize? Equality in possessing the same divine essence and attributes is unlikely, since deity was something he always had. Equality of status is more likely. Although he possessed full deity, he was not equal with the Father in human recognition. Nor was this recognition something he tried to forcefully seize.

Instead **he emptied himself.** Christ, who possessed all the divine attrtibutes and who had equal status with God, "emptied himself (*heauton ekenosen*)." The emphatic position of *heauton* ("himself") and active indicative verb indicate that this act of "emptying" was voluntary on the part of the preexistent Christ. Of what he emptied himself has been widely debated. Kenotic theories abound (Greek *ekenōsen*). Much depends on how the following participle *labōn* ("taking") is understood. Some understand the aorist participle as defining an action subsequent to that of the main verb "emptied": "He emptied himself and then took the form of a servant." However, this leaves open the question of what he emptied himself. Opinion is wide-ranging, including: He emptied himself of his (1) essential divine attributes, (2) relative attributes, (3) divine prerogatives, (4) divine glory (outward manifestation of deity) or (5) divine wealth (the riches of living in the divine presence). However, the aorist participle could also define not *of what* but *how* he emptied himself (modal use): He emptied himself **by taking the form of a servant**. The following aorist participle *genomenos* would then explain **the form of a servant** as **being born in the likeness of human beings** (*en homoiōmati anthrōpōn genomenos*). Theologically, however, this is not to say that he only appeared human much like angels can take the form of a human being, while their form is spiritual (Docetism). Church history judged this view as heretical. He was *fully* a human being (or "incarnate").

To be noted is Ralph Martin, who favors reading *ekenōsen heauton* not as "he emptied himself" but rather "he poured himself out." He gave up all thought of self and poured out his fullness to enrich others. It is a poetic, hymn-like way of saying that Christ put himself totally at the disposal of people.[14]

The possession of divinity and humanity and their exact relationship gave rise to three church councils. There was agreement that the Son was divine. However, the phrase **who existed in the form of God** (*en morphē theou*; v. 6) raised the question: "Existed when?" The Arian controversy involved the notion that the Son was created by God the Father in time and substance. There was a time when the Son did not exist. This was countered by a theological formulation at the Council of Nicaea (AD 325), which became known as the Nicene Creed. It declared that the Son was co-eternal and con-substantial (*homoousion*) with the Father.[15] There was never a time when he was not a person ("co-eternal") and possessed a divine nature (*homoousion*).[16]

The phrase **in the likeness of human beings** (*en homoiōmati anthrōpōn*, v. 7) also raises the question of the nature of this human likeness. Did the Son become a human being or merely add a human nature to his divine one? Were there two persons with two distinct natures?

One must have a great deal of respect for the theological challenges that the Incarnation posed for the church in the early centuries AD. The idea of two persons—God the Son and Jesus, with two distinct natures, one divine and one human, was tackled by the Council of Chalcedon (AD 451). Athanasius proposed that "he is God from the essence of the Father begotten before time and that he is human from the essence of his mother, born in time; completely God, completely human. He was equal to the Father as regards divinity and less than the Father as regards humanity."[17] How the divine and human co-existed was termed *hypostasin* or one person with two natures. There was no blending of two natures but a distinct co-existence (or hypostasis) of the two in one person. The council declared that in Christ there are two natures with each retaining its own properties and

14. Martin and Hawthorne 2004: 117.

15. The Nicene Creed (Greek: Σύμβολον τῆς Νικαίας or, τῆς πίστεως, Latin: Symbolum Nicaenum) is a statement of belief widely used in Christian liturgies. It is called Nicene because it was originally adopted in the city of Nicaea (present day İznik, Turkey) by the First Council of Nicaea in 325. In 381, it was amended at the First Council of Constantinople to add the Holy Spirit. The amended form is referred to as the Nicene or the Niceno-Constantinopolitan Creed. See Mirbt 1911: 640–42.

16. Kelly 2006.

17. Athanasius, *C. Ar.* ch. 23.

together united in one person (*hen prosōpon*) and one single subsistence (*mian hypostasin*).

Kai ("and") introduces a further idea. An aorist participle *heuretheis* ("found") *precedes* the main verb, thereby defining a prior action: **And after he found himself in the form of a human being, he humbled himself.** The main verb ("he humbled himself") is then *followed by* an aorist participle (*genomenos*). If the aorist participle defines a coordinating action, then the sense is: "He humbled himself *and* became obedient until death." However, the participle could again be modal *how* he humbled himself, namely, by experiencing death as the ultimate human end: **He humbled himself** by **becoming obedient to death, even death by crucifixion** (v. 8).

Christ's sacrificial death by crucifixion had results. What he didn't try to seize, namely, the universal recognition of being worthy of worship and possessing divine equality, he received, when he was **elevated**. Some translate the Greek *hyperypsosen* as "highly exalted." However the term means to regard a person as being exceptionally honored in view of high status (L&N). **Elevated to the place of highest honor** is thus a more accurate rendering. Elsewhere Paul equates this **honor** with Christ's ascension to God's right hand (Eph 1:26; Col 3:1; cf. Mark 16:19; Acts 2:33; 7:55–56). It is noteworthy that he was given **the name above every other name**. In Greek thought one's "name" did not distinguish one person from another but said something about a person's character and status.[18] However, it was not the name "Lord" as one would expect but the name **Jesus.** It is **at the name of Jesus** that **each and every knee will bow**. The response to the name **Jesus** elicits worship. To bend the knee was a sign of religious devotion to someone (L&N).

Some scholars argue that *tō onomati 'Iēsou* does not mean that everyone will bow "at the name Jesus," but that everyone will bow at the name given to Jesus, namely, "Lord" (*kyrios*).[19] However, verse 11 states that **every tongue will confess that Jesus Christ is Lord**. Here **Lord** refers to his status or **place of highest honor.** It is the name *Iēsous* that causes universal worship. The Hebrew term *Jeshua* (or "Joshua") transliterated *Iēsous* means "salvation."[20] This ties back to the idea of God incarnate. Divinity took on

18. Hans Bietenhard, "ὄνομα" *TDNT* 5:242.

19. Martin argues that the reason Paul places the name of Jesus here is because by doing so he is saying that lordly power has been put into the hands of the historical person of Jesus of Nazareth. He is not some cosmic cipher or despotic ruler but a figure to whom Christians could give a face and a name. Martin 2004: 126–27.

20. The word "Jesus" is the Latin form of the Greek *Iēsous*, which in turn is the

full humanity, namely, **Jesus,** whose sinless sacrifice on the cross secured our salvation. That sacrifice earned him the worship and public acknowledgment **that he is Lord.** The name **Jesus** is also a recognition of his full humanity in addition to his full deity. Indeed "Jesus Christ is Lord" was the earliest confession of the church (Acts 2:36; Rom 10:9; 1 Cor 11:23; 12:3; 16:22).

The hymn encapsulates what Peter preached at Pentecost (Acts 2:36) that God made Jesus, whom the people crucified, Lord and Messiah. There is a universal dimension. **God the Father** appointed him sovereign over the universe: **Each and every knee in heaven, on earth and under the earth** will bow to him. God the Father also made him the object of universal worship: **And every tongue will publicly acknowledge that Jesus Christ is Lord**. The end result is that God the Father is glorified: **to the glory of God the Father.** The Greek *doxa* refers here to the manifestation of God's excellence, power, and majesty (Anlex).

Fusing the Horizons: Philippians 2:6–11 The Model of Christ

The Philippian hymn in verses 6 to 11 presents Christ as the example of the selflessness and sacrificial giving that Paul has been urging the Philippians to show toward those inside and outside the church. Although one might argue that this is Christ's divinity at work, it is not. It is his humanity. During his earthly life he was as fully human and open to temptation as we are: "For we do not have a high priest who is unable to sympathize with our weaknesses, but we have one who in every respect has been tested as we are, yet without sin" (Heb 4:15). Paul himself calls the Corinthians to "imitate" him as he "imitates Christ" (1 Cor 11:1). While the hymn is theologically rich, Paul's motive is not theological but ethical. His intent is not to provide a creedal statement but rather Christian living instruction. He does this by appealing to Christ as the ultimate model of how we should behave.

This means that in the final analysis Pauline authorship of the hymn is not important. What is important is that Paul saw it as the perfect model of Christian living for the church. Unlike models today that encourage climbing the ladder of success regardless of whom one steps on in the process or by putting forward one's credentials as superior to others, Christ's example is just the opposite. He indeed did possess the credentials of divinity and a position

---

transliteration of the Hebrew *Jeshua*, ("Joshua"), meaning "salvation." See BDAG s.v.

worthy of the highest honor (v. 5). However, instead of claiming or fighting for the honor due him, Christ assumed the lowliest of positions. Instead of climbing the proverbial corporate ladder, Jesus descends it.[21] He waived his divine rights and took on the form of a servant by being born in the likeness of human beings. And after he found himself in the form of a human being, he humbled himself by becoming obedient even to death by crucifixion.

Like too many Christians today, some in the Philippian church were ambitious, considering themselves as superior to others. They sought to promote themselves and get ahead regardless of the Christian toes on which they stepped. To this end they justified doing and saying whatever was in their best interests. In part this was because of outside opposition and influences. In Phil 1:27–28 Paul instructs the church: "Whether I come and see you or only hear about you in my absence, I will know that you stand firm in one spirit, contending as one person for the faith of the gospel without being frightened in any way by those who oppose you." By putting forward the example of Christ, Paul challenges both first-century Roman Imperial and twenty-first century values. While we may value our human citizenship, we must keep in mind that "our citizenship is in heaven from which we receive a Savior, the Lord Jesus Christ, who will transform our humble body to be conformed to his glorious body by the powerful work that only God can accomplish" (3:20–21).

---

21. See Hellerman 2005: 129–63 on *carmen Christi* as *cursus pudorum*. He rightly argues that instead of Christ climbing the *cursus honorum*, he descends the *cursus pudorum* or "course of shame." *Cursus honorum*, or "course of honor" was the required sequence of public offices that a young Roman aristocrat was to follow as he advanced in his career. At each stage the upwardly mobile young man gained new responsibilities and new privileges. Lower classes of people, both inside and outside of Rome, developed their own sequence of offices that mimicked the upper classes. Hellerman argues that the concern for such honor ratings and status was, if anything, greater than normal in Philippi, because the elites in Philippi were Roman and the city was a Roman colony often called "little Rome."

Excursus: The Philippian Hymn

Philippians 2:6–11 has generated more scholarly literature than any other portion of Paul's letters.[22] As such it warrants special attention. The primary issues concern authorship, structure and genre, and theology.

Authorship

Scholarship is divided over whether verses 6 to 11 are an early Christian hymn or composed by Paul himself. Majority opinion favors an early Christian hymn. Those who support Pauline authorship argue that Paul composed verses 6 to 11 in a spontaneous burst of inspiration and label them "exalted prose" (versus a hymn).[23] However, the non-Pauline vocabulary and distinctive theology point to a pre-Pauline text used in early church worship.[24] The vocabulary of these verses includes words only found here in the New Testament: *harpagmon, katachthoniōn, morphē,*and *hyperypsōsen.* There are also theological concepts that are unique to these verses. "He emptied himself" (v. 7), "taking on the form of a slave" (v. 7) and (3) "born in the likeness of human beings" (v. 7) do not appear elsewhere in the New Testament. God elevating him and giving him the name that is above every other name (v. 9) is also unique. The universal element ("every voice"), comprehensive location ("in heaven, on earth and under the earth") and the confession that Jesus Christ is Lord (vv. 10–11) are distinctive. On the other hand, the key Pauline theological ideas of redemption and resurrection that appear elsewhere in the letter are missing here.

There are also several non-poetic phrases that need explanation: "Even death by crucifixion" (v. 8), "in heaven, on earth and under the earth" (v. 10) and "to the glory of God the Father" (v. 11). Martin proposes that these

---

22. See Bakken 1968; Bockmuehl 1997; Bornkamm 1959; Boyer 1979; Dawe 1962; Dibelius 1915; Dupont 1950; Fee 1992; Feuillet 1965; Finley 1973; Furness 1958–1959; Furness 1967–1968; Georgi 1964; Gibbs 1971; Glasson 1974–1975; Gundry 1994; Hammerich 1966; Harvey 1965; Helmbold 1974; Hofius 1976; Hooker 1975; Howard 1978; Hudson 1965–1966; Hurtado 1984; Jeremias 1964; Käsemann 1968; Lambrecht 2003; Lohmeyer 1976; McClain 1998; MacQuarrie 1974; Marshall 1968; Martin 1997; Moule 1953; Murphy-O'Connor 1976; Peppard 2008; Seeley 1994; Streiker 1964; Strimple 1979; Thomas 1970; Thomas 1975; Wilson 1976; Wright 1986.

23. Fee 1992: 29–46. Compare Gundry 1994: 288 and Wright 1992: 56–57.

24. Hansen 2009: 122, 127–31.

are Pauline redactions to a preexisting hymn.[25] Hurtado speaks of "Paul's adaptations to a Christian hymn."[26]

On balance, the overwhelming number of non-Pauline elements and hymnic features point to Paul's use of an early church hymn. The Christology of preexistent divinity, the incarnation of being born a human being as well as the ultimate humiliation of death by crucifixion fit Pauline theology. However, verses 9 to 11 about Christ's elevation to the position of Lord and the appropriateness of bowing the knee in worship, which do not fit the concerns of Paul's letter, suggest that he was inserting a preexisting piece that he kept intact except perhaps for the three additions noted above.

Structure and Genre

The structure of verses 6 to 11 is also debated. For some this lack of consensus shows that the line between exalted prose and a hymn are too fine to be definitive about the genre.[27] Of the scholarly proposals, there are three that have the most support.

Lohmeyer argues for six stanzas with three lines in each stanza. It is of note that the Nestle-Aland Greek text editions follow Lohmeyer's structure:[28]

1. *hos en morphē theou hyparchōn* (who, though existing in divine form)

   ouch harpagmon hēgēsato (did not regard as something to be grasped after)

   to einai isa theō (equal status with God)

2. *alla heauton ekenōsen)* (Instead he emptied himself)

   morphēn doulou labōn (taking the form of a servant)

   en homoiōmati anthrōpōn genomenos (being born in the likeness of human beings)

3. *kai schēmati heuretheis hōs anthrōpos* (and finding himself in the form of a human being)

   etapeinōsen (he humbled himself)

25. Martin 2004: 101–2.
26. Hurtado 1984: 101.
27. See Hawthorne 1983: 77.
28. Lohmeyer 1976: 4.

genomenos hypēkoos mechri thanatou thanatou de staurou (becoming obedient to death even death by crucifixion)

4. *dio kai theos auton hyperypsōsen* (Therefore God elevated him to the place of highest honor)

   kai echarisato autō (and gave him)

   to onoma to hyper pan onoma (the name above every other name)

5. *hina en tō onomati 'Iēsou* (that at the name of Jesus)

   pan gony kampsē (every knee will bow)

   epouraniōn kai epigeiōn kai katachthoniōn (in heaven, on earth and under the earth)

6 *kai pasa glōssa exomologēsetai* (and every tongue will acknowledge)

   hoti kyrios 'Iēsous Christos (that Jesus Christ is Lord)

   eis doxan theou patros (to the glory of God the Father)

Martin puts forward the structure of six stanzas each consisting of a couplet. He brackets three phrases as Pauline additions.[29]

- *hos en morphē theou hyparchōn* (who, though existing in divine form,)
  ouch harpagmon hēgēsato to einai isa theō (he did not regard equal status with God as something to be grasped after)

- *alla heauton ekenōsen* (Instead he emptied himself)
  morphēn doulou labōn (taking the form of a servant)

- *en homoiōmati anthrōpōn genomenos* (being born in the likeness of human beings)
  kai schēmati heuretheis hōs anthrōpos (and finding himself in the form of a human being)

- *etapeinōsen heauton* (he humbled himself)
  genomenos hypēkoos mechri thanatou [*thanatou de staurou*] (becoming obedient to death [even death by crucifixion])

- *dio kai theos auton hyperypsōsen* (Therefore God elevated him to the place of highest honor) *kai echarisato autō to onoma to hyper pan onoma* (and gave him the name above every other name)

- *hina en tō onomati Iēsou* (that at the name of Jesus)

pan gony kampsē [epouranōn kai epigeiōn kai katachthoniōn] (every knee will bow) [in heaven, on earth and under the earth]

- *kai pasa glōssa exomologēsetai* (and every tongue will acknowledge)

hoti kyrios Iēsous Christos [eis doxan theou patros] (that Jesus Christ is Lord [to the glory of God the Father])

On the basis of the theological theme, Jeremias proposes three stanzas with four lines in each stanza:

Preexistence

hos en morphē theou hyparchōn (who, though existing in divine form,)

ouch harpagmon hēgēsato to einai isa theō (he did not regard equal status with God as something to be grasped after)

alla heauton ekenōsen (Instead he emptied himself)

morphēn doulou labōn (taking the form of a servant)

Incarnation

en homoiōmati anthrōpōn genomenos (being born in the likeness of human beings)

kai schēmati heuretheis hōs anthrōpos (and finding himself in the form of a human being,)

etapeinōsen heauton (he humbled himself)

genomenos hypēkoos mechri thanatou [thanatou de staurou] (becoming obedient to death [even death by crucifixion])

Exaltation

dio kai theos auton hyperypsōsen (Therefore God elevated him to the place of highest honor) *kai echarisato autō to onoma to hyper pan onoma* (and gave him the name above every other name)

hina en tō onomati Iēsou pan gony kampsē [epouraniōn kai epigeiōn kai katachthoniōn] (that at the name of Jesus every knee will bow [in heaven, on earth and under the earth])

kai pasa glōssa exomologēsetai hoti kyrios Iēsous Christos [eis doxan theou patros] (and every tongue will acknowledge that Jesus is Lord [to the glory of God the Father])

Critics have pointed to Jeremias' need to eliminate the three bracketed phrases above for structural fit. If, however, one sees these three phrases as Pauline additions to an existing hymn, then Jeremias proposal has much merit. Despite the criticism, his delineation of stanzas by theological theme is appealing.

It is worth noting that hymn stanzas throughout the centuries have been ordered theologically. The earliest known Christian hymn *Phos Hilaron* is recorded by an unknown author and found in *The Apostolic Constitutions*, which is commonly dated c. AD 375–380.[30] There it appears in a collection of songs sung in the morning, in the evening, before meals, and at candle lighting. *Phos Hilaron* was sung at the lighting of lamps in the evening and has therefore been known as the "Lamp-Lighting Hymn."[31]

Phos Hilaron was the first complete example of an ancient Christian hymn. It too was divided into twelve verses, varying between four and eleven syllables per verse. Basil the Great (AD 329–379) spoke of the singing of the *Phos Hilaron* as a cherished tradition of the church.[32] The hymn was already considered old in Basil's day.[33] *Phos Hilaron* is the earliest known extra-biblical Christian hymn that is still being used today. The hymn is featured in the *Vespers* of the Orthodox Church:[34]

> *O Gladsome Light*
> *Of His holy glory*
> *Of the Immortal heavenly Father*

30. *Britannica Online* 2019, "Hymn," http://o-www.search.eb.com.library.uor.edu:80/eb/article-9041781.

31. *Phos Hilaron* was first translated ino English by the nineteenth-century poet Henry Wadsworth Longfellow.

32. *De Spiritu Sancto* 29.73.

33. The earliest fully preserved text is dated c. AD 200 or earlier.

34. *Byzantine Catholic Church* 2006: https://mci.archpitt.org/Publications2.html

Holy, blessed Jesus Christ
Now we have come to the setting of the sun
And behold the light of evening
We intone Father, Son, and Holy Spirit Divine
Worthy at all times to sing hymns
With voices of praise
O Son of God
Giver of Life
Therefore the world glorifies Thee

Although structural proposals of Phil 2:6–11 vary, this does not necessitate calling these verses "exalted prose" rather than a hymn. The hymnic elements are undeniable and differ from the non-literary prose of the first-century letter that precedes and follows verses 6–11. There are the telltale signs of a hymn. With only one or two small changes, it can stand alone as an independent composition. The relative pronoun *hos* ("who") is typical of a religious hymn as are the participles *hyparchōn, labōn, genomenos,* and *heuretheis.* The vocabulary is rich. The Greek term *harpagmon* is a graphic word to describe something done suddenly and powerfully (BDAG). There are also the superlatives *to onoma to hyper pan onoma* (*beyond* every other name) and *hyperypsōsen* (exalted to the *highest* level). There is the parallelism found in all forms of poetry. In verse 7 lines *morphēn doulou labōn* ("taking the form of a servant") and *en homoiōmati anthrōpōn genomenos* ("being born in the likeness of human beings") appear to be synonymous. Verse 8 is structured along the lines of a synthetic parallelism, where the first line *etapeinōsen heauton* (he *humbled* himself) is expanded in the second line *genomenos hypēkoos* (becoming *obedient*) and further expanded with *mechri thanatou* (*to the point of death*) and even more so in the final phrase *thanatou de staurou* (death by crucifixion).[35]

There is also paradox. He who is fully God becomes fully human (vv. 6–8). He who received the death penalty and was executed by the mode Romans saved for the most heinous of crimes (*crucifixion*) was honored with the most exalted of statuses (*Lord*). Verses 9 to 11 build to a climax. God elevates him, all humankind worships him, and all humankind publicly acknowledges that Jesus Christ is *Lord.*

Although some would dispute the importance of viewing verses 6 to 11 as a hymn with poetic elements and dramatic features, failure to do so impacts interpretation. If treated as prose (albeit elevated), meaning can be

35. See: https://en.wikipedia.org/wiki/Category:Poetic_devices.

read into and questions asked of the text that would not be appropriate for a poetic genre. For example, the question, "Of what did he empty himself?" is moot, if answered by the following participles: "*by taking* the form of a servant" and "*by being born* in the likeness of human beings." Similarly, if "the form of a servant" and "in the likeness of human beings" are understood to be parallel ideas, then it would be inappropriate to interpret each separately. Equally important is the need not to squeeze theology out of poetry. "Each and every knee will bow and every tongue publicly acknowledge" can't be pressed to support universal salvation. Nor can "in heaven, on earth, and below the earth" be pressed to support Christ's descent into Hades (or Hell) to save the dead.

Theology

Equally debated is the theological interpretation of key phrases of verses 6 to 9. Striking differences of opinion in the early centuries resulted in various church councils. See above. The three most debated phrases are as follows:

- Existing In The Form of God
- Not Regarding Equality With God As *Harpagmon*
- He Emptied Himself

Existing In the Form of God

The first issue is what is meant by Christ existing "in the form of God" (NRSV *en morphē theou hyparchōn*). There are no less than five competing interpretations. Much depends on the lens through which this phrase is interpreted.

The Greek Classical Philosophy Lens: Read through the lens of Greek classical philosophy, *en morphē theou* denotes possessing the divine essential attributes. Christ possessed the divine *ousia* (substance).[36] One difficulty is that one must ignore the preposition *en*. The text does not state "He was God" as in John 1:1 (*theos ēn*). Nor does it say that Christ had "the form of God." The text is not *morphē theou* but *en morphē theou*. Christ "existed in the form of God." Some attempt to circumvent the problem by translating the phrase as "he who participated in the being and shared in the essence

---

36. See Lightfoot 1953: 110; Bruce 1989: 45; Hawthorne 1983: 84; Fee 1992: 204–5.

of God."[37] However, the range of meaning for the verb *hyparchō* does not include "participate" or "share." Instead *hyparchō* is commonly used as a synonym of the verb "to be" (*einai*). The meaning of *hyparchō* is "'to be in a state or circumstance, be'; as a widely used substitute in Hellenistic Greek" (BDAG). Also, "participation in" begs the question of the extent or manner in which Christ participated in the divine attributes. The parallel phrase *morphēn doulou labōn* ("taking the form of a servant") raises even more questions about the nature of Christ's "participation." Was Christ fully human or did he merely don a human form?

The LXX Lens: Read through the lens of the LXX, *morphē theou* denotes possession of the *glory* of God (*doxa*), that is, his visible form. The proposal is that Christ "wore the garments of divine majesty."[38] Commonly cited in support are John 17:5 ("So now, Father, glorify me with the glory that I had in your presence before the world existed") and Heb 1:3 ("He is the reflection of God's glory"). There are also the numerous references in the LXX to the glory of God as his outward appearance. This outward appearance is typically a manifestation of earthly power. The "glory of the Lord" was a cloud that descended on Mt. Sinai (Exod 24:16), covered the tabernacle (Exod 40:34–35; Num 9:16) and filled the temple (1 Kgs 8:11; 2 Chr 7:2; Ezek 10:4). The "glory of the Lord" thunders (Ps 29:3) and appears as fire (Num 9:15–16).

One difficulty with this interpretation is that, while God's glory appears as a cloud, thunder, fire *et alia*, nowhere is Christ's glory manifested in this way. The transfiguration could be understood as an outward manifestation of God's glory (although the term is not used): "And he was transfigured before them, and his face shone like the sun, and his clothes became dazzling white" (Matt 17:2). Also, Christ does perform miracles and engage in non-human acts such as walking on water, calming a storm and the like. In addition, Paul does refer to God giving Christians "the light of the knowledge of his glory, which is in the face of Christ" (2 Cor 4:6) and to the Spirit transforming Christians into "ever-increasing glory" (2 Cor 3:18).

However, Christ prays that the Father glorify him with his *preexistent* glory (John 17:5). Since God is spirit, what exactly are these preexistent "garments of divine majesty"? Moreover, the parallel *morphēn doulou labōn* can not be understood as "the glory (*doxa*) of a servant (or slave)." Servants and slaves in Greco-Roman culture had no majesty. Also *en morphē theou*

---

37. Lightfoot 1953: 133.

38. O'Brien 1991: 210–11; Wannamaker 1987: 185–87; Strimple 1979: 260–61.

hyparchōn is equated with *to einai isa theō* or "equality with God," which points more toward Christ having the same divine attributes. "Majesty" may be a divine attribute but it is not the only one.

The Adam/Christ Lens: Read through an Adam/Christ lens, *en morphē theou* (as well as the entire hymn) is understood in light of a first Adam-second Adam theology found elsewhere in Paul (Rom 5:18-19; 1 Cor 15:45-47). The first Adam was created "in the image and likeness of God" (Gen 1:26-27), while the second Adam innately bore "the image of God" (2 Cor 4:4; Col 1:15). Also, while the first Adam attempted to become like God (Gen 3:5-6), the second Adam did not regard equality with God something to be grasped after (i.e., exploited; Phil 2:6b).[39] The first Adam became "a living being," while the last Adam became "a life-giving Spirit" (1 Cor 15:45). The first Adam was from the earth (Gen 2:7), while the second Adam (Christ) was from heaven (1 Cor 15:47). While we now bear the image of earthly Adam, in the future we shall bear the image of the heavenly Adam (1 Cor 15:49).[40]

The Adam/Christ lens further equates *morphē* with *eikōn* ("image"). This too involves outward appearance. There is Pauline support. Paul refers to God's image and connects it with "glory" in 2 Corinthians. "The gospel's light displays the glory of Christ, who is the image of God" (2 Cor 4:4). Christians are being transformed into the same image by the Spirit (2 Cor 3:18). In Colossians God's image is connected with the Son: "The Son is the image of the invisible God, the firstborn over all creation" (Col 1:15).[41]

However, this understanding falters at the same points. Christ preexisted "in the form of God" (*en morphē theou*). He did not preexist in the "image" of God. It was during his earthly ministry as a human being that he reflected the image of an invisible God (Col 1:15).

A Gnostic/Hellenistic Religions Lens: Read through a gnostic/Hellenistic religions lens, the entire hymn is about Jesus as a descending-ascending savior figure derived from the gnostic redeemer myth. Gnostic theology posits an imperfect spirit, who was the God of Abraham. The true God is distant and not easy to know. This myth says that humans are divine souls trapped in the ordinary material world. To get free from this world, a person has to get *gnosis* or secret redemptive knowledge, which is given

---

39. Dunn 2003: 114-21; Hooker 1975: 152-53; Dibelius 1915: 75; Wright 1992: 57-60; Hurtado 1984: 122.

40. Furness 1967-1968: 181; Hooker 1975: 160-64; Jervell 1960: 203-4.

41. See Bird 2009: 51-52.

only to an elect few. Christ is called the "heavenly man" and *en mophē theou* is his divine mode of being (which he shares with the inscrutable God).[42] He descends to redeem humanity from their material prison and ascends back to heaven.[43]

There are few current proponents of this interpretation. The difficulty is the lack of similarity between the gnostic redeemer myth and the details of Phil 2:6–11. It is true that the hymn begins with a divine being. However, this divine being is *born* as a human being (the Incarnation), *dies* on a cross, and is *elevated* by God to the position of "Lord." The dissimilarities are profound.

The Divine/Human Condition Lens: Read through the lens of the divine/human condition, *en mophē theou* refers to Christ possessing the "condition" or "status" of divinity. He held a unique place within the divine life and existed in a divine condition and status. The value of this understanding is that it fits with the following "equality with God" (v. 6b) and with *morphēn doulou labōn* (v. 7). He who from the beginning had equal status with God and existed in a divine condition, chose to identify himself with humanity and to accept the human condition and status. Tob 1:13 is used in support: "Then the Most High gave me [Tobit] favor (*charin*) and status (*morphēn* "a good standing") with Shalmaneser" (NRSV and most translations).[44]

This is an attractive option. It is the option that fits best with Christ's contrasting modes and conditions in his preexistent (v. 6) and human (v. 7) states. However, extra-biblical usage of *morphē* with the meaning "condition" or "status" is lacking. LSJ lists "form, shape" and "outward appearance" as meanings in Hellenistic Greek.

Conclusion: The most tenable position is that "existing in the form of God" refers to fully possessing the divine attributes. Although he fully possessed the divine attributes, he did not possess equal status, that is, there was no universal human recognition of his divine status. This fits best with fully possessing the divine attributes, but not grasping after the human recognition that God the Father possessed throughout Israel's history.

42. The discovery of the *Nag Hammadi* documents led scholars such as Rudolph Bultman to propose a pre-Christian gnostic influence on New Testament Christianity. See Bultmann 1951: 193; Reitzenstein 1978: 357–58; Howard 1978: 368–87.

43. See the critique by Käsemann 1968: 66–67, 72, 78–80 and Georgi 1964: 263–33. See also Murphy-O'Connor 1976: 25–50; Talbert 1967: 141–53; Jervell 1960: 227–31; Collange 1979: 97.

44. See Martin 1967: 96; Jervell 1960: 230–31; Collange 1979: 97.

This recognition is only achieved through his elevation to the position and status of "Lord" to whom worship is the appropriate human response. The primary objection noted above is the presence of the preposition *en*. However similar phraseology is found in Col 2:9, where Paul states: "All the fullness of divinity dwells *in him* bodily" (*en autō katoikei pan to plērōma tēs theotētos sōmatikōs*). Existing *en morphē theou* can readily be understood along the same lines as "all the fullness of divinity dwells in him [Christ]." Even in Col 2:9, "bodily" can be understood as "really," "in reality" in contrast with "in mere appearance" (L&N 8.2).[45]

Not Regarding Equality With God As *Harpagmon*

The second theological issue is what is meant by *ouch harpagmon hēgēsato to einai isa theō*. The Greek term *harpagmon* is only found once in the Greek Bible (Job 29:17). In extra-biblical texts both active and passive meanings are found (LSJ). The active meaning is to "snatch," "seize," or "rob" (Plutarch, *Mor.* 2.12a). Its passive sense is that which is "seized," "exploited," or "taken advantage of" (Anlex). It can denote "prey" or "plunder" that is seized as in Job 29:17: "I broke the teeth of the wicked person and made him drop the prey (*harpagma*) out of his mouth." It can also refer to a positive outcome of the seizure, namely, a "prize" or "windfall" (BDAG).

The active meaning of "snatch" or "grab at" has supporters. For Hooker it was the fact that Christ did not "snatch at" divine equality with God as Adam did.[46] She sees it as a reference to Gen 1:26 and Adam's being created in God's image. For Christ, as for Adam, the prize was not yet possessed but desirable. Just as Adam grasped after equality with God (Gen 3:5), so too Christ could have done so (as the second Adam). The preexistent Christ was not equal with God but could have seized it had he chosen to do so.[47]

However, this implies that divinity was not something that predated the Incarnation. It was Christ as a human being that sought divine status. Yet verse 6 states that, prior to the Incarnation, he "existed in divine form" and possessed "divine equality with God." This has led the majority of current scholarship to support the understanding that Christ possessed the

---

45. Hawthorne supposes that, since Paul as a Jew would be a strict monotheist, he would be unable to bring himself to say, "Christ is God." Instead he expressed this reality in the circumspect language found in Phil 2:6.

46. Hooker 1975: 151–64.

47. So Dunn 2003: 120–21; Hoover 1971: 95–119. See also Knox 1948: 229–49.

right to hold on to his divinity and to use it to his own advantage should he choose to do so.[48] However, he did not choose this route. He put aside his highly prized divinity.[49] He refused to act selfishly and use his divine rank and privilege for his personal advantage.[50]

A recent publication by Katherine Shaner argues for the meaning "robbery" and situates the Philippian hymn in the cultural context of the Roman imperial practice of rape and robbery. She argues that Aphrodisian reliefs and female images sexualized women's bodies to depict conquered peoples. Rather than something to be exploited or grasped, *harpagmon* means "rape and robbery." Verses 6 to 11 depict the power of divine emperors (rather than Christ's preexistent divinity).[51]

Understanding the participle *hyparchōn* as causal "*because* he existed in the divine form" (rather than concessive "although") has led some to an alternative interpretation. Christ did not grasp after equality with God *because* he already possessed it. Instead he humbled himself by not taking advantage of what he already possessed ("divine majesty and rule") and assumed the human form of earthly mortality and servanthood ("human mortality and one who serves").[52] It was precisely *because* he possessed divinity, that he reckoned equality with God not as a matter of getting but of giving.[53] This interpretation has the appeal of making a theological statement. God by nature was not that of a grabber but, rather, that of a giver.[54]

A preferable option is to treat the participle as *concessive: Although* he fully possessed the divine attributes ("he existed in divine form") and could have claimed and taken advantage of "equal divine status," he chose not to grasp after his rightful status (human acclaim). Instead he humbled himself (the opposite) and took on human status (that of a servant versus one who deserves to be served) and human form(being born in human likeness). This reading acknowledges his pre-incarnate fully divine existence and status and his post-incarnate fully human existence and refusal to use his divinity to his advantage.

48. Hoover 1971: 118. Compare Hansen 2009: 146.

49. Lightfoot 1953: 111.

50. Silva 2005: 103; Cf. "He did not exploit his status as cosmic creator" (Martin 1976:143).

51. Shaner 2017: 342–63.

52. Compare Wright 1986: 345; O'Brien 1991: 215–16; Hoover 1971: 118.

53. Moule 1970: 271–74; Hawthorne 1983: 85.

54. See Furness 1967–1968: 178–82.

He Emptied Himself

The third theological issue is what is meant by *alla heauton ekenōsen*. This text has been one of the most researched and theologically debated. The typical question is of what one, who had equality with God, emptied himself. (For the church councils' debate, see above.)

The verb form *kenoō* occurs five times in the New Testament. In 1 Cor 1:17 it means to cause someone to be emptied of power: "In order that the cross of Christ may not be *emptied of its power*." In 1 Cor 9:15 it is used of depriving someone of something: "I would rather die than have someone *deprive* me of my ground for boasting." In 2 Cor 9:3 it refers to taking away the significance of something or to make invalid:"I am sending the brothers in order that our boasting about you may not *prove to have been invalid*." In Rom 4:14 the passive is used with the sense to make null or void: "If it is the adherents of the law who are to be the heirs, faith is *null* and the promise is void." In each of these four passages, the action taken is clear. In Phil 2:7 it is not. The major proposals are six in number.

Divestiture: An early proposal was that Christ emptied himself of his divine attributes, humbled himself, and took the form of a servant. This meant that the Incarnation involved stripping himself of his divinity and becoming a mere human being (versus adding a human nature to his divinity). However, this conflicts with what follows in verses 9–11. If verses 9–11 are seen as a reversal, it is the reversal of Christ's status from servant to Lord that is depicted and not a restoration of his divinity. Verse 6 states that he possessed equality with God prior to and after the Incarnation. He simply chose not to use it to his advantage.

A more recent proposal is that of a modified divestment, although opinion varies on the question: "Of what did he divest himself?" Some suggest that he divested himself of his relative attributes of omniscience, omnipresence, and omnipotence.[55] Others suppose that he divested himself of his divine glory (outward manifestation of deity). Still others think that he divested himself of the riches of living in the divine presence.[56]

However, even modified divestment opinions are difficult both in terms of the context and the grammar. The main verb is the indicative aorist *ekenōsen*, which is followed by a series of participles. If a sequence of actions was intended, one would expect an aorist participle followed by a

55. Lightfoot 1953: 112,
56. Plummer 1919.

series of verbs: *"After* he emptied himself, he took the form of a servant and was born in the likeness of a human being. Instead we have a verb followed by participles. This syntax is commonly used when mode is indicated: *How* did he empty himself, instead of, *of what* is then the question. "He emptied himself *by taking* the form of a servant and *being born* in the likeness of a human being. This syntax is followed by an aorist participle, an indicative verb, and another aorist participle. With this sequence the aorist participle commonly defines an action prior to that of the main verb: "*After* he found himself in the form of a human being, *he humbled* himself *by becoming obedient* to the point of death, even death by crucifixion" (vv. 7–9).

He Poured Himself Out: An alternative proposal is to equate "he emptied himself" with Christ putting himself totally at the disposal of others.[57] There is abundant theological support for Christ's sacrificial conduct. The language of being "poured out like a drink offering on the sacrifice and service of your faith" occurs in Phil 2:17. Self-sacrifice also fits the broader context. In contrast to those at Philippi who were demanding their rights and insisting on their own way, Christ set aside his rights and privileges to serve others. "He humbled himself" is the motif of this entire passage. However, there is no lexical support for the verb *kenoō* meaning "poured out" except in the literal sense of emptying an object such as a pitcher or bowl.

He Took the Form of a Slave: Some point to the cultural parallel between Christ taking the form of a slave and the Greco-Roman slave, who had no rights. Christ went from possessing everything to having nothing. As in 2 Cor 8:9 Christ became "poor" so that we might become "rich."

A slight twist in this understanding is that "he emptied himself" is figurative for making himself nothing. He had everything (divine equality) but became nothing, expressed figuratively as "taking the form of a slave."[58] For example, at the Passover meal, Christ got up, took off his outer clothing, and wrapped a towel around his waist. Then he poured water into a basin and began to wash his disciples' feet, drying them with the towel that was wrapped around him (John 13:4–5). Some even propose a literal understanding. Christ became a slave to God.[59]

He Subjected Himself to Elemental Powers: A further proposal is that Christ gave up a heavenly existence and limited himself by becoming

57. Furness 1967–1968: 93–94; Hawthorne 1983: 85.

58. Silva 2005: 104.

59. Hurtado 1984: 113–26.

human. In becoming a human being, he also became enslaved to the demonic powers of sin, death, and the Law. He submitted himself to these powers until his death through which he freed himself and humanity from their captivity (Rom 8:2–3).[60] However, nothing in the hymn supports such an understanding. God elevated Christ from that of an obedient servant to the position of *Lord*. Nothing is said about God freeing him from human slavery to the elemental powers of sin, death, and the Law.

Became a Righteous Martyr: Some put "he emptied himself" in the context of Jewish martyrology from the Maccabean period. Christ "emptied himself" by taking on the role of a righteous man and loyal servant of Yahweh, who suffers for his loyalty. The Zealots during Jesus's time saw themselves as following in the line of the Maccabees, who fought and died for the honor of God as his righteous warriors.[61]

"Christ Fulfilled Isaiah's Vision of A Coming Servant of the Lord": Taking the form of a servant" is understood as fulfilling the role of the Servant of the Lord in Isa 42:1–4; 49:1–6; 50:4–7, and 52:13–5:12. Supporters of this position are many.[62] "He emptied himself" is equivalent to, "He poured out himself to death" (Isa 53:12). His reward was to be "highly elevated by God and given the name that is above every name . . ." (Phil 2:9–11). Similar language is found in Isa 52:13: "See, my servant shall prosper; he shall be exalted and lifted up, and shall be very high."[63] There is much to commend this interpretation. Some object to understanding *doulos* as a "servant" versus a slave. However, Paul calls himself a *doulos* of Christ in the letter openings of Rom 1:1, 1 Cor 1:1, and Titus 1:1. Yet virtually all translators render the term as "servant." Paul undoubtedly uses the term as a self-description with the meaning of one who has totally submitted himself to Christ (BDAG).

The Outcomes of a Christ-Like Mind: (2:12–18)

> [12]Therefore, my beloved, just as you have always obeyed not only in my presence but now even more in my absence, keep working together for your preservation and safety with a sense of awe. [13]God is he who is also working among you both to will and to

60. Käsemann 1968: 45–88; Jervell 1960: 229.

61. Schneider, "σχῆμα," *TDNT* 7:956.

62. See especially Fee 1995: 212; Longenecker 1970: 105; Hansen 2009: 50; Gundry 1994: 271–94; O'Brien 1991: 221–24.

63. Martin 1976; Jeremias 1963.

work for his good pleasure. [14]Do everything without grumbling and arguments. [15]This way you will be blameless and without guile. You will be God's children without blemish in the midst of a crooked and twisted generation in which you shine like stars in the world. [16]By holding fast to the Word of life, you will be my boast at the time Christ returns and show that I neither ran nor labored in vain. [17]But even if I am poured out on the sacrificial altar and service for your faith, I will be glad and rejoice with all of you [18]and you with me.

Paul now tells his converts what their role is to be in light of Christ's sacrifice and current Lordship. **Therefore, my beloved, just as you have always obeyed** is not an overstatement or a ploy on Paul's part to force their obedience. The Philippian church had a special place in Paul's affection. **My beloved** indicates as much. Elsewhere Paul refers to a church as beloved by God (e.g., Rom 1:7) or as his beloved children (e.g., 1 Cor 4:14; 10:14). However, in no other letter does he repeatedly emphasize his love for a particular congregation. Earlier he said that he "longed for them with the affection of Christ" (1:8). Two chapters later he calls them "my joy and crown whom I love and long for" (4:1). Undoubtedly this is because the Philippians have listened to Paul with unquestioned deference. This kind of deference is rare. They have also followed Paul's instructions **not only in** his **presence but even more in** his **absence.** However, now Paul is in prison facing trial and his opponents are capitalizing on his situation to undermine his footing at Philippi. Plus, there is disagreement within their ranks. In light of external opposition and internal dissension, Paul gives two commands:

- Keep working together for your preservation and safety with a sense of awe (*meta phobou kai tromou tēn heautōn sōtērian katergazesthe*; v. 12)

- Keep doing everything without grumbling and arguments (*panta poieite chōris gongysmōn kai dialogismōn*; v. 14)

The Greek is commonly translated: "Work *out* your salvation with fear and trembling." However, this is misleading. It suggests that each individual gains salvation through works. Paul elsewhere argues strongly against just such a notion. "We are saved by grace through faith and not by works" (Eph 2:8, 10). Salvation by God's grace makes Christianity distinctive from every other world religion.

The first thing to note are the plural pronouns. Paul is speaking of a corporate work. Earlier he instructed them not to be focused on *self* interest but on *others'* interests. Satan's strategy is to divide and conquer. Paul's strategy is to unite and conquer. Hence **work together** versus "work it out yourself" is a preferable translation. The goal is not "salvation" but **preservation**. The larger context indicates that *sōtēria* does not carry the eschatological sense of salvation through effort. The Greek word *sōtēria* has a range of meanings, including "deliverance," "preservation," and "safety" (L&N). The verb Paul uses, *katergazesthai*, has the sense of working at something until it is brought to completion ("to effect by labour," "to achieve," "to accomplish," LSJ). Paul's command is not an aorist *work out* but a present tense *keep working together*, which emphasizes the need for continuous effort. The call, therefore, is to stop fighting and **keep working together** (as they have been) to keep the congregation safe. How they are to do this is with "fear and trembling" (NRSV). Again, this translation can be easily misunderstood. Paul is not picturing God as a dictator before whom they must grovel in fear. Nor is he referring to a future judgment-induced obedience. It is true that Paul refers to the future event of appearing "before the judgment seat of Christ" (2 Cor 5:10). However, the judgment in 2 Cor 5:10 entails an *individual* (versus corporate) accounting of our earthly behavior as a Christian.

In light of Paul's next statement, the phrase in Phil 2:12 is better understand as **with a sense of awe: For God is he who is working among you both to will and to work for his good pleasure** (v. 13). This is sometimes translated "in you" and taken as "in *each* of you," whereas the Greek is plural **among you,** that is, corporately. The term for "work" is different. The Greek verb is not Paul's previous *ergazesthai* but *energein*, from which we get our English word "energy." It is a favorite word of Paul's (18x). God is the Great Energizer Bunny (as it were) that keeps on going. He has great determination **to will** and he has great energy **to work. To will** does not refer to God commanding our obedience but to his own determination to be involved in our progress. Determination and energy is what God brings to the job. But he also takes pleasure in doing so (*hyper tēs eudokias*). Some interpret *eudokia* as "that good will to which Paul desires the Philippians to attain."[64] However, the grammatical sequence is "God is he, who is working among you AND wills AND works **for his good pleasure**." God is the subject of the sentence. The singular article *tēs* functions as the possessive

---

64. See, for example, Hawthorne 1983: 101.

pronoun "his."[65] Reference to the congregation requires a plural article. The sense here is "to do according to what pleases him" (L&N). There is human responsibility. The Philippians need to expend effort. There is also divine responsibility. God is at work to get them to the finish line. Plus it pleases him to do so (**for his good pleasure**).

To effect a good result, the Philippians must abandon their bad attitude. There is to be no more grumbling and arguing (v. 14). This accomplishes nothing. The term **grumbling** (*gongysmōn*) is commonly used of Israel's response during the wilderness years. It is used to express discontent ("to complain," "grumble," "complain" [L&N]). That there were strongly expressed differences of opinion among the Philippians is evident from Paul's firm request "that Euodia and Syntyche be of the same mind in the Lord" (4:2). The singling out of these two women indicates that they exercised leadership and influence as Paul's **co-workers in the ministry.**

Moving forward as a united front against strong opposition is essential. The result of such unity is unique to this letter: **This way you will be blameless and without guile. You will be God's children without blemish in the midst of a crooked and twisted generation** (v. 15). Paul holds them to a very high standard:

- Blameless
- Without guile
- Without blemish

To be **blameless** means that no one could point a finger at them. Their conduct couldn't be faulted by others: "So that no one can criticize you" (NLT). Paul himself stated that his conduct toward the Thessalonians was **blameless** (1 Thess 2:10). To be **without guile** translates the Greek word *akeraios* or "unmixed," "not polluted." It was used of undiluted wine, unalloyed metal, and pure blood lines. When used of people, it denotes a character marked by integrity and innocence of evil (LSJ). They are also to be **God's children without blemish.** If a person belongs to God's family, they reflect God's character and so share the family characteristics. The Greek word *amōma* is used in the Old Testament of the requirement that an animal presented to God be "without blemish" and hence worthy of God (Lev 14:10; Num 6:14).[66]

---

65. Greenlee 1986: 22.
66. See Frederick Hauck, "ἄμωμος," *TDNT* 4:831.

Blameless, without guile, and without blemish are set in contrast to Greco-Roman society, which Paul describes as **crooked and twisted.** **Crooked** is the Greek medical term *skolios* (scoliosis) or curvature of the spine. It refers to those who are "unscrupulous and dishonest" (L&N). Peter urged his Jewish listeners: "Save yourselves from this crooked generation" (Acts 2:40). Whether Greek or Jew, first-century society as a whole was unprincipled. It was also **twisted** (*diestrammenēs*), a Greek medical term for twisted or distorted vision (LSJ). Both Peter and Paul probably have LXX Deut 32:5 in mind, where it is said of Israel: "His people have acted corruptly toward God. The spot on them is not that of His children but of a crooked and twisted generation" (*genea skolia kai diestrammenē*).

By contrast the Philippians are called **to shine like stars.** Though *phōstēr* may refer to any light-producing object, it is used especially of any light-producing object in the sky, such as the sun, moon, and other planets (L&N). In this case, the Philippians are to be shining lights in a dark world. The key to being a light-bearing people of integrity is **by holding fast to the Word of life.** There are a number of ways that the Greek phrase can be translated. "Holding fast to the living word" is common. This would then be a reference to the word of God, the Scriptures. However, given Paul's reference to heavenly luminaries, he might be thinking of Christ as the Word of life. In this case, John 1:1–5 comes to mind: "The Word was God. All things came into being through him. What has come into being in him was life, and that life was the light of all people. The light shines in the darkness, and the darkness did not overcome it."

Paul shifts to athletic language. If the Philippians are **holding fast to the Word of life,** Paul will be able to **boast at the time Christ returns** and know that he has **neither run nor labored in vain** (v. 16). If they fall short, Paul has no basis for boasting in them at Christ's return. Paul's **boast** is not personal. The sense is that they are Paul's pride and joy much as children are their parents' pride and joy. If, however, they fall short, then Paul will **have run and labored in vain. Run** (*trechō*) is the Greek term for a footrace and the grueling training that goes into it. The word **labor** (*kopiaō*) is found frequently in Paul to describe the gospel ministry as "hard work." Jesus's disciples say: "We worked hard all night long and caught nothing" (Luke 5:5). Paul similarly refers to the labor involved in using goats' hair to make tents and outdoor items as "hard work and toil" (2 Thess 3:8). The exertion of a foot race, and the hard work of manual labor will be for naught, if the Philippians do not cross the finish line with Paul.

Paul turns to sacrificial language: **Even if I am poured out on the sacrificial altar and service for your faith.** The verb *spendein* is a cultic term for a drink offering. What Paul has in mind is the Old Testament wine offering that is poured over the sacrifice.[67] Use of a drink offering is found elsewhere only in 2 Tim 4:6, where the reference is to martyrdom: "For I am already being poured out like a drink offering, and the time of my departure is at hand." In both instances the drink offering represents the offering up of life. Paul pictures a Roman legal verdict of death as being poured out on a sacrificial altar. As a drink offering is poured out at the foot of the altar, the apostle sheds his blood.[68]

Even given a verdict of death, Paul states that he will **rejoice** and the Philippians will **rejoice** with him. **I will be glad and rejoice with all of you and you with me.** The terms "joy" and "rejoice" appear four times in verses 17 to 18. Suffering for the gospel of Christ—whether it be Paul or the Philippians, is a cause for rejoicing. Four of Paul's twelve uses of "joy" and "rejoicing" are found here. "Rejoicing" as a response to persecution and opposition is an important theme in Paul's letters and especially here in his letter to the Philippians. Opposition does not mean that God has abandoned them. It merely confirms that their lives and their words stand out over against their society, thereby exposing the elite for the corrupt leaders that they are.

Fusing the Horizons: Facing Adversity

As Christians our job today is no less of a challenge. We too face a morally bankrupt global society. Hate speech abounds. Decency is hard to come by. Tragedy is politicized. Accusations of "treason" and calls for leaders to resign abound. Those who stand up for integrity and truth are ridiculed and often labeled as the villains. This is particularly true of Christians, who are called homophobic, islamophobic, sexist, racist, and a host of other names. Some wonder if justice is possible, especially at the highest levels of our key institutions. Indictments and lawsuits are the norm. The average citizen and blue collar worker is disparaged. Our administrators are kicked out of restaurants, bullied at their homes, and harassed by the media.

---

67. The act consisted of pouring the wine on (*speiseis ep' autou*) the altar, God's table, or on the burnt offering. See LXX Exod 30:9; Num 28:24.

68. Otto Michel, "σπένδω," *TDNT* 7:528.

The easier path is to remain quiet and not raise any red flags. Also easier is to lash out at those among us over differing opinions abozut how to handle social upheaval. Yet, like the Philippians, we too are called to put aside our differing opinions and unite as children of light. Like the first-century Christians, we are called to shine the light of truth and goodness in our society.

There is no room for grumbling and arguing. This accomplishes nothing. The call is for harmony, selflessness, and good will toward others. The "good will" to which Paul desires the Philippians to attain, should be the hallmark of a Christian community. The famous pink energizer bunny that keeps going and going has become a "symbol of longevity, perseverance and determination" says Mark Larsen, communications category manager for Energizer. In the past decade, everyone from politicians to sport stars have used the Energizer Bunny to describe their staying power.[69] It is long overdue that Christians become known for these same qualities and to herald our God as the one and only Energizer.

Travel Plans and Upcoming Visits: 2:19–30

[19]Now I hope in the Lord Jesus to send Timothy to you soon so that I too am cheered by news about all of you. [20]For I have no one who is as like-minded as Timothy. He is genuinely concerned about you. [21]All the rest focus on their own interests and not on the interests of Jesus Christ. [22]You know his proven character. He has been like a son to me and served with me in the work of spreading the Gospel. [23]Therefore I hope to send him as soon as I see how things turn out for me. [24]I am confident in the Lord that I too will come soon. [24]Finally, I find it necessary to send Epaphroditus back to you. [25]He is my brother, co-worker and fellow soldier. He is also your messenger and servant for my needs. [26]He has been longing for all of you and in great distress because you heard that he had become ill. [27]Indeed he nearly died. However God had mercy on him and not only on him but also on me so that I would not have unbearable grief.[28] Therefore I made haste to send him to you so that after you saw him again, you would rejoice and I would be free from sorrow. [29]So welcome him in the Lord with much joy and hold those like him in high esteem. [30]For on account of the work of

69. www.EnergizerHoldings.com.

Christ's Gospel, he came close to dying, risking his life to fill your
lack of service to me.

Notification of an upcoming visit is a central part of the first-century letter. However, it usually appears in the closing section of the body of the
letter just prior to final greetings and farewell.[70] That Paul moved his travel
plans to this point in the letter suggests strategic importance rather than the
typical newsy information. Add to this the sheer length of the travel plans.
Paul devotes 12 of 104 verses (12 percent) to this topic. The travel plans are
those of:

- Timothy (vv. 19–23)
- Paul (v. 24)
- Epaphroditus (vv. 25–30)

Paul gets one verse, while Timothy and Epaphroditus split the balance. The
extent to which Paul expands his notification of travel plans provides an
insight into both the concerns of Paul as well as those of the Philippians.

Timothy

Paul informs the Philippians that he **hopes to send Timothy** to them **soon**.
The church had sent Epaphroditus with funds to meet Paul's needs and to
offer support during Paul's imprisonment (4:18). However, Epaphroditus's
return was delayed due to an illness that was a near-death experience. The
Philippians were facing severe opposition themselves and in need of support. This explains the sending of Timothy to provide this support. It also
explains Paul's concern to get **news about** them. He assumes that it will be
good news so that he is **cheered** by the information he receives. The Greek
term *eupsychō* ("cheered") is only found here in the New Testament, but it is
frequent in first-century letters with the meaning "of good courage," "stout

70. See, for example, Romans, 1 Corinthians, Ephesians, Colossians, Philemon. Some
conclude that the mention of travel plans signal the end of one letter (3:1a) and the beginning of another (3:1b; or perhaps interpolations). However, 1 and 2 Corinthians also
include travel plans earlier in the letter. This is the case when travel plans serve a strategic
function in addressing problems. In the case of 1 Corinthians, Paul states in ch. 4 that he
will be coming soon and will discipline those who say that he has abandoned them. In 2
Corinthians, news of travel plans occur in ch. 7 in response to Titus's return with news of
the church. Also, Paul's letters were dictated. News could have arrived during a pause in
dictation that motivated Paul's apparent outburst. See Culpepper 1980: 350; Doty 1979:
36–37, 43; White 1971: 143–45; and Belleville 1986: 15–37.

of heart" (LSJ). This may be motivational strategy on Paul's part. Several of Paul's letters include the statement "confident of your obedience" following news of his travel plans. It is Paul's diplomatic way of telling a church to clean up their act before he or his emissary arrive. In the case of the Philippians, the need is for the church to stop arguing and present a united front before Timothy arrives.

Paul provides a lengthy list of Timothy's credentials. This is odd, given that Timothy was involved in planting the church at Philippi (Acts 16). If Paul's imprisonment is in Rome c. 60–62 (as most scholars argue), it has been over ten years since that founding visit. Even so, what Paul lists would have already been known to them. However, if Timothy was being sent to address **grumbling and arguments** (v. 14), then a repeat of his credentials would be a good reminder. This must have been difficult for Paul, since he couldn't come at this time and address these problems himself. What Timothy brings to the table are a **like-mindedness** (*isopsychon* "of equal soul," "feeling," "mind" [BDAG]), a **genuine concern**, **proven character**, and service with Paul in **the work of spreading the gospel** (v. 22).

In short, Paul has no one of the same mind, who is genuinely concerned for the church. The others **focus on their own interests and not on the interests of Jesus Christ.** Paul shifts to what he thinks to what they know. **You know his** *dokimēn*, a term that refers to learning the genuineness of something by examination and testing (L&N). Timothy underwent a period of testing that proved he was truly genuine and the Philippians were witnesses to **his proven character**. Timothy was also **like a son** to Paul. Paul typically refers to his converts and ministry colleagues as "sons." However, there is more here. Timothy was one of Paul's converts (Acts 16:1–3), who was trained by him and was a co-worker throughout Paul's missionary travels. However, **like a son to me** points to a familial relationship. It says that Timothy cared for Paul as a son would care for his own father. Hence Timothy knows Paul's mind better than anyone else, and for this reason Paul is sending him to Philippi.

Paul

In the meantime, Paul stays put, while he awaits the outcome of his trial. Yet, he is confident in the Lord that he too will travel to Philippi (v. 24).

Epaphroditus

Given the prevalence of highway robberies, one wonders if the church became concerned about Epaphroditus because of the funds he was carrying on his person. Paul lists his credentials like he does for Timothy. **He is my brother, co-worker and fellow soldier** and his job description was to be **your messenger and servant for my needs.** Paul's emphasis on his **haste to send him to** them, his command to **welcome him in the Lord with much joy** and his instruction **to hold those like him in high esteem** suggest some sort of concern about how the church would receive him. There is also the repeated reference to how **ill** he had been, coming **close to dying,** and **risking his life.** Just in case the church was reluctant to give him a hero's welcome, Paul does a bit of arm twisting, noting that Epaphroditus risked **his life to fill your lack of service to me.** This is underlined by Paul's repeated references to **being free of** sorrow once he knows that they had welcomed Epaphroditus on his return.

Brother indicates that Epaphroditus was a Christian. The church is family with brothers and sisters like a human family. **Co-worker** (*synergon*) is the term Paul uses of someone who ministers side-by-side with him. **Fellow soldier** (*systratiōtēn*) is "one who experiences great hardships along with us" (L&N). The last descriptive suggests that Epaphroditus's illness was the result of hardship that was linked to Paul's imprisonment. **Risking his life** to help Paul out is elsewhere only used of Priscilla and Aquila: "Great Prisca and Aquila, my **co-workers,** who **risked their lives for me**" (Rom 16:3). **Servant** (*leitourgias*) is not the term used of a slave or household servant. It is used of one performing a public service (Anlex). In the Greco-Roman period, the term was used to describe the priesthood and the sacrificial system. Thus Paul is viewing Epaphroditus's service to him as a religious one.[71] **Your messenger** is a bit weak. It is the term *apostolos* with the meaning "ambassador" or "envoy" (LSJ). Paul emphasizes this role by mentioning it twice. The second time (v. 30), it is set in contrast to the Philippians' **lack** of service to him.

Paul mentions three times that Epaphroditus was **ill** and nearly **died.** Epaphroditus' **distress** and Paul's own **grief** appear twice in the space of seven verses. Paul also mentions **God's mercy** on both Epaphroditus and himself. This suggests perhaps that without God's intervention, Epaphroditus would have died. The only letter that comes close to the language

71. Strathmann, "λειτουργός," *TDNT* 4:219–22.

of these verses is Philemon. In the case of Philemon, Paul advocated for welcoming back his slave Onesimus as a **brother**, who appears to have been in Rome on business for Philemon. There is the suggestion that Onesimus had planned on staying in Rome and using the funds that he had in his possession. Epaphroditus was also caring funds from the Philippian church to use on Paul's behalf. Perhaps Epaphroditus' delay in returning raised a similar concern.

News, however, was sent (how we don't know) that his delay was due to a near-fatal illness. Therefore, Paul assures the church that Epaphroditus **has been longing** for them and in **great distress** himself about the church receiving news of his illness. It is very difficult to read between the lines and reconstruct the Philippians' half of the conversation. We know nothing about Epaphroditus apart from Paul's words here. It could be that his delay in returning was perceived as a selfish disregard for the strong opposition and persecution that the church was facing. This would explain why Paul finds **it necessary** (literally "compels him" [LSJ]) **to send Epaphroditus back, made haste** to do so, and why doing so would release Paul **from sorrow**. It also fits with Paul's rebuke at the start of chapter 2 that the church was selfishly focusing on its own interests and not the interests of others such as Paul and **the work of Christ's gospel**.

Fusing the Horizons: Valuing our Leaders

How difficult it must have been for Paul not to be able to travel to Philippi and help his beloved church handle opposition from without and within. The leaders were fighting (4:2). Church members were arguing (2:1–4). However, Epaphroditus' recovery meant that he could at least send a trusted colleague and church leader to deal with the problems at Philippi. Just how stressed Paul had been for both Epaphroditus' and the church's well-being is clear from his language. God delivered Paul from "wave upon wave of grief" (*lypēn epi lypēn*) in the healing of Epaphroditus. Sending him to Philippi meant "less anxiety" (*alypoteros* comparative) regarding the church.

Pastors and leaders face equal stress today. To be pastor of a church is typically a lonely job. It is the rare church that cares for their pastors and leaders. Very often there is criticism and two-faced behavior. There is definitely a lack of privacy. I recall an intern and his family having church members look through their windows to see what they were doing and criticize the intern's capability to lead the church. One wonders if the Philippians were questioning Epaphroditus' illness. Was he ill-prepared for what faced him in Rome? Could he not stand the strain? Gossip in my opinion is the number-one hindrance to a healthy church. Perhaps this is why Paul goes out of his way to employ extravagant praise and to command the church to welcome him in the Lord with much joy and hold those like him in high esteem.

We live in a society today that does not tend to esteem its leaders. Violent and vocal protests have been increasing. Baseless accusations that destroy a leader's reputation are becoming the norm. This norm has been spilling over into our churches. Christians refuse fellowship with one another due to political differences. Leaders claiming to be Christians resort to the most vile of verbal attacks to win support and elections. The self-sacrificing character of Paul, Timothy, and Epaphroditus is sorely needed in our churches and in our society today. There are still heroes among us, who should also be held in high esteem.

Philippians 3

The Goal of Knowing Christ Versus Human Achievements: 3:1–9

[1]Now for the rest, my brothers and sisters, keep on rejoicing in the Lord. For me to write these things to you is not bothersome but a way to keep you on firm footing. [2]Keep watching out for the dogs. Keep watching out for those evil workers. Keep watching out for those who mutilate the flesh. [3]For we are the circumcision, those who worship God spiritually and boast in Christ Jesus rather than placing our confidence in human credentials. [4]If some think they have confidence in human credentials, I do too and even more. [5]Circumcised on the eighth day after birth; of the race of Israel; of the tribe of Benjamin; a Hebrew of Hebrews. [6]According to the Law, a Pharisee; according to zeal, a persecutor of the church; according to righteousness, blameless in keeping the Law. [7]But whatever I counted as gain, I have now come to regard as loss because of Christ. Indeed, I continue to regard everything as loss because of the surpassing value of knowing Christ Jesus my Lord. [8]Because of him, I have suffered the loss of everything and reject everything as so much rubbish so that I gain Christ. [9]Thus I will be found in him, not having my own righteousness based on the Law but that which is through faith in Christ—a righteousness from God based on faith.

The Greek *to loipon* commonly translated "finally" leads us to think that Paul is drawing to a conclusion. Yet, two chapters remain. Some understand this protracted finale to be either an interpolation or a second letter that was inserted at this point. This has partly to do with the translation "finally." The term can also be translated **now for the rest** (LSJ) or "well then."[1] The understanding that Paul is drawing to a conclusion is also due to the common mistranslation of three Greek imperatives as commands to start doing something versus to keep doing something. Phil 3:1–2, 17 are typically translated: "Rejoice in the Lord" (v. 1), "Watch out for the dogs" (v. 2), and "Imitate me" (v. 17). "Watch out for the dogs" in particular seems then to appear out of nowhere. However, translating Paul's imperatives as present tense commands sheds a different light.

- Keep on rejoicing in the Lord (v. 1)
- Keep watching out for those who mutilate of the flesh (v. 2)
- Keep on imitating me (v. 17)

A present tense translation assumes that they are already doing what Paul highlights. He merely emphasizes the need to keep on doing it. The need to rejoice instead of arguing was Paul's emphasis in chapter 2. The need for unity in the face of opposition and persecution has been equally emphasized.

For me to write these things to you is not bothersome but a way to keep you on firm footing points forward and not backwards. It was common in the concluding section of the letters of Paul's day to reiterate the reason for writing. However, Paul's typical conclusion is "I, Paul, write this with my own hand" (1 Cor 6:21; Gal 6:11; 2 Thess 3:17; Col 4:18; Phlm 20). Paul takes the pen from his secretary and writes the final greeting in his own hand for purposes of authentication. The secretary of Romans pens his own greeting: "I, Tertius, the writer of this letter, greet you in the Lord" (Rom 16:22). **For me to write these things to you** is unusual as a letter closing element but fits well as an opening to further instruction. Paul's concern is **to keep** them **on firm footing.** The Greek term *asphales* means to keep secure and safe (LSJ).

Keep on rejoicing in the Lord is Paul's first command (v. 1). **Rejoice** is the major theme of the letter. A call to "rejoice" and the term "joy" are found fifteen times in the letter's four chapters (1:4, 18, 25; 2:2, 17 (4x), 18, 28, 29; 3:1; 4:1, 4, 10). No other letter has this many occurrences. **Keep watching out for the dogs** is Paul's second command (v. 2). The Greek term is not that of an indoor pet. It is the outside dogs that run in a pack, prowling about the garbage and rubbish thrown into the streets. **Dogs** here is a metaphor. To call a Jew a "dog" was the ultimate insult. Jews considered dogs

---

1. Moule 1953: 161–62.

as well as pigs to be unclean animals. Comparable words today would be "scum," "filth," or "trash." **"Dogs"** was used in Athenian circles of the Cynics. The label referred to the Cynics' rejection of conventional manners and their decision to live on the street (Aristotle, *Rhet.* 3.10.1411a25). However, Paul's **evil workers** were not Greeks but Jews **who mutilate the flesh** or as Phillips translates: "Be on your guard against those curs, those people who do evil, who seek to mutilate the body." "Mutilate" (*katatomē*) only occurs here in the New Testament. It is a contemptuous word for circumcision.[2] In Rom 2:28–29, Paul states: "For he is not a Jew who is one outwardly, nor is circumcision that which is outward in the flesh. He is a Jew who is one inwardly and circumcision is that of the heart, in the Spirit, not in the letter." Circumcision was a rite of passage and an identity marker for Jews as members of God's covenant people. Paul had nothing against circumcision. He himself was circumcised and had Timothy circumcised for ministry purposes (Acts 16:3). Paul is referring here to Jews who claimed the name of Christ yet followed him around, telling the Gentiles that they had to become a Jew (and be circumcised) before they could become a Christian (Acts 15:1; "Judaizers"). The Old Testament sense of circumcision as a symbol of Israel's covenant with God was replaced by the new covenant in Christ, which is marked by circumcision of the heart (Rom 2:29) and the indwelling of God's Spirit (1 Cor 3:9; 6:19) versus external Law obedience.

While Paul states that circumcision and non-circumcision are matters of indifference in the church (Gal 5:6), what Paul takes issue with is the fact that Judaizing Christians placed their confidence in the "flesh" (human achievement) and not "in Christ" (divine accomplishments). Judaizers boasted in what they had achieved and so undermined the total sufficiency of what Christ accomplished on the cross on our behalf. Even more, they not only took pride in their own religious standing but sought to improve the standing of others through circumcision and a person's religious accomplishments. It is to place **confidence in human credentials** (Phil 3:3). Instead, Paul states that **we** (the church) **are the circumcision.** For those who are truly circumcised **boast in Christ Jesus** and not in human achievements. Similarly to **worship God** (*latreuontes*) was not to attend to the performance of specific religious rites or rituals as found in both Jewish and Greco-Roman temple services (L&N). Instead Paul claims that to truly **worship God** is to worship **spiritually.** For God is Spirit and desires to be worshiped in Spirit (John 4:23–24).

2. Helmut Köster, "κατατομή," *TDNT* 8:110.

According to Paul, "a person is a Jew who is one inwardly, and real circumcision is a matter of the heart—it is spiritual and not literal. Such a person receives praise not from others but from God" (Rom 2:28–29 NRSV).

It is not that Paul was speaking out of envy for what he himself lacked. Paul states that he has seven better reasons for placing confidence in the flesh than anyone else had: **If some think they have confidence in the human credentials, I do too and even more** (v. 4):

- Circumcised on the eighth day after birth
- An Israelite
- Of the tribe of Benjamin
- A Hebrew of Hebrews
- A Pharisee
- Zeal
- Righteousness

To be **circumcised on the eighth day after birth** meant to be born into a law-abiding Jewish family (v. 5). "You shall circumcise the flesh of your foreskins, and it shall be a sign of the covenant between me and you. Throughout your generations every male among you shall be circumcised when he is eight days old" (Gen 17:11–12). Jesus' parents circumcised him in accordance with the Law. **Of the race of Israel** is someone born to Jewish parents (versus converted) and thereby possessing all the rights and privileges of God's covenant with Israel. **Of the tribe of Benjamin** was a tribe of prestige. This was the tribe who gave Israel her first king (1 Sam 9:1–2). Mordecai proudly claimed Benjamin as his tribe (Esth 2:5). Only Benjamin remained loyal to David and his successors (1 Kgs 12:21). They along with Judah made up the nucleus of the new colony of Jews who returned to Jerusalem after the Exile (Ezra 4:1). **A Hebrew of Hebrews** meant that Paul was brought up to speak the mother tongue and was educated "strictly according to our ancestral law" and at the feet of renowned Rabbi Gamaliel (Acts 5:34; 22:3). **According to the Law, a Pharisee** (v. 6). The Pharisees were held up as models of piety in Jesus' day. They were noted for their strict adherence not only to Mosaic Law (written law) but also to scribal interpretations (Oral Law). Josephus claimed that the Pharisees received the full support and goodwill of the common people in contrast to the more elite Sadducees, who were of the upper class.[3] The Pharisees were influential members of the Sanhedrin, Israel's highest court. Indeed, Paul used this credential to his advantage before the Sanhedrin: "Brothers, I am a Pharisee, a son of Pharisees. I am on trial concerning the hope of the resurrection of the dead" (Acts 23:6). **According to zeal,** Paul was **a persecutor of the church**. Paul claims that no one was more zealous for the Lord's honor than he was. He hunted down Christ followers and brought them to Jerusalem to be tried as heretics before the Sanhedrin. Such zeal was a mark of the Maccabean family, who refused to bow the knee to the gods of their Greek northern rulers (the Seleucids).[4] The Maccabean patriarch, Mattathias, killed a Jew, who stepped forward to sacrifice to a Greek idol. He also killed the Greek officer, who was sent to enforce the sacrifice. This sparked a revolt that ended in eighty years of independence for Judea (1 Macc 2:1—16:24).

Lastly **according to righteousness,** Paul was **blameless in keeping the Law**. Paul obeyed it perfectly. He had kept all the commandments from his youth up. He lived a totally blameless life at which no one could point a critical finger. **Righteousness** (*dikaiosynē*) in this instance means conformity to external rules that are considered to be the requirements of God. This included far more that the Decalogue. Mosaic Law numbered 613 commandments that were accepted as normative among practicing Jews.[5] The fact that Paul declares that he was **blameless** in observance of Mosaic Law indicates that he was a most remarkable Jew.

While Paul had every reason to be confident and proud of his heritage and religious accomplishments, his response was the opposite: **But whatever I counted as gain, I have now come to regard as loss because of Christ** (v. 7). **Gain** (*kerdos*) and **loss** (*zēmia*) are the language of accounting with a column marked "assets" and a column marked "liabilities" (MM). Paul already used the term **gain** earlier. For Paul to live is to preach Christ but to die is personal **gain** (1:21). The idea of balancing the scales of profit and loss was also part of Jewish thinking. Even Jesus used it: "For what will it profit them if they gain (*kerdēsē*) the whole world but forfeit (*zēmiōthē*) their life?" (Mark 8:36). The main verb *hēgēmai* (**regard**) is in perfect tense. It indicates that Paul gave his stellar privileges a lot of thought and reached a settled decision. They were of no advantage compared with **the surpassing**

3. Josephus, *Ant.* 13.5.9.

4. Eisenberg 2015: 3–332.

5. Havlicek and Morcineck 2016: 33–49.

value of knowing Christ Jesus my Lord. *Zēmia* ("loss") is not the objective loss of the thing itself. It is the subjective loss of its value. Paul still had all his privileges and accomplishments on record. However, everything that was once valuable has now lost its value for Paul.

Paul's further response is surprising. Such privileges of birth and upbringing and such spiritual achievements and accomplishments, Paul **continues to regard** (now present tense) **as loss** and **rejects everything as so much rubbish** (v. 8). The Greek "rubbish" (*skybala*) is a vulgar term for what one throws into the garbage or onto a dung-heap (LSJ). Paul's accomplishments are not merely an accounting loss but something he views with disgust compared with **knowing Christ**. The believer has only one privilege and achievement of spiritual worth, namely, the privilege of knowing Christ. **Knowing Christ** is more than an acquisition of facts or knowledge of a creedal confession. To know Christ is to know a person. Nor is this an instantaneous knowledge. It is one that continues to grow until the time that we meet Christ face-to-face.

To gain Christ, Paul states, is to **be found in him not having my own righteousness** based on Law obedience but **a righteousness through faith in Christ** (v. 9). The Greek phrase *tēn dikaiosynēn tēn dia pisteōs Christou* is debated. The two primary interpretations are: (1) righteousness gained through the believer's faith in Christ and (2) righteousness gained through Christ's own faithfulness. The issue is whether righteousness is based on our faith in Christ or in Christ's own earthly faithfulness. There are several factors that support of "faith in Christ." The contrast in chapter 3 is between a righteousness achieved through human law obedience and one that is based on faith. The preposition *ek* here is key. The righteousness that Paul affirms is a **righteousness** *ek theou* (from God) and *epi tē pistei* (based on faith). The righteousness that he now rejects is a righteousness *ek nomou* (from the Law) and *echōn emēn* (based on human achievement). In short, the contrast is between "faith" and "works of the Law." It is a righteousness from God which is based on faith versus a righteousness which is from the Law and based on human achievement. Rom 3:21–22, 28 is a close parallel:

> "But now, apart from the law, the righteousness of God has been disclosed, and is attested by the law and the prophets, the righteousness of God through faith in Jesus Christ (*dia pisteōs 'Iēsou Christou*) for all who believe. For there is no distinction, ... For we hold that a person is justified by faith apart from works prescribed by the law (*pistei chōris ergōn nomou*)" (NRSV).

Fusing the Horizons: The Goal of Knowing Christ Versus Human Achievements

In Paul's day those who placed confidence in Jewish religious achievements were called "Judaizers." Today we might label them as religious legalists. These are those who put in the "assets" column the religious requirements and achievements of their particular denomination or local church. Today it might include:

- Baptism
- Confirmation
- Growing up in a religious family
- Attending Christian schools
- Tithing 10 percent of one's income
- Faithful worship
- Abstaining from drinking, playing cards, attending movies, and dancing.

These are the privileges of birth and upbringing and of spiritual achievements. Some claim to be more religious than most. They give more than 10 percent. They attend Sunday School as well as the worship service. They sing in the choir, serve on a board or committee, and volunteer in their community. "Whatever was to my profit," Paul says, "I now consider loss." "Whatever was to my profit" is what I place value on or whatever makes me look good. What then should believers put under the assets column of their spiritual balance sheet? What should we treat as of value in the Christian life? For Paul "knowing Christ" was the only asset of value. Knowing Christ is not so much head knowledge as it is heart knowledge. To know Christ is to be in a relationship with him. Getting to know someone means spending time with them, delighting in their company, wanting to know what they think and value, and desiring to talk with them. A number of hymn writers knew something of this experience: "Oh what a friend we have in Jesus" (Joseph Scriven). "Jesus lover of my soul, let me to thy bosom fly" (John Wesley). "Jesus, Jesus, Jesus. Sweetest name I know. Fills my every longing. Keeps me singing as I go" (Luther Bridgers); "Turn your eyes upon Jesus. Look full at his wonderful face. And the things of earth will grow strangely dim. In the light of his glory and grace" (Helen Lemmel). Self-worth for the believer comes through knowing Christ and not through privileges of birth and up-bringing or through our spiritual achievements and religious accomplish-ments. The goal of the Christian is get to know Christ better. That is Paul's goal and it should be ours as well.

Pressing Toward the Goal: 3:10–14

> [10]To know him and the power of his resurrection. To participate in his sufferings and be conformed like him in his death. If thereby, I will attain to the resurrection of the dead. [12]Not that I have already attained it or have already reached the goal. But I pursue it so as to take hold of that for which I was taken hold of by Christ. [13]Dear friends, I myself do not consider that I have attained it. But this one thing I do. I forget what lies behind me and strain forward to take hold of what lies ahead. [14]I pursue the goal to receive the prize of God's heavenly calling in Christ Jesus.

Paul goes on to show what else is in the "gain" side of the column. The language is hymnic:

> To know him [Christ]
> And the power of his resurrection
> To participate in his sufferings
> And be conformed like him in his death
> If thereby I will attain to the resurrection of the dead

The poetic character of the strophes makes unpacking Paul's exact meaning difficult. If one takes the strophes in historical order **the power of his resurrection** would refer to Pentecost and the outpouring of the Spirit, empowering the disciples (including Paul), to perform miracles, healings, exorcisms, and the like. Paul himself states that it was "by the power of signs and wonders, by the power of the Spirit of God, I have fully proclaimed the good news of Christ from Jerusalem and as far as Illyricum" (Rom 15:19). To p**articipate in his sufferings** ([*tēn*] *koinōnian* [*tōn*] *pathēmatōn autou*) is commonly translated "and [know] the fellowship of his sufferings." How-ever, the Greek *koinōnia* is typically used in the New Testament of "par-ticipation" with the implication of financial support or ministerial activity (L&N). The Greek *pathēmatōn* refers to a suffering, calamity, or misfortune that befalls one (LSJ). The sense is not that Paul is completing sufferings that Christ left uncompleted. This would be to say that Christ's sacrifice was not sufficient to procure our salvation. Sufferings similar to what Jesus endured throughout his ministry is what is likely in view. Paul provides a lengthy list of his ministerial sufferings in 2 Cor 11:24–29:

> Five times I have received from the Jews the forty lashes minus one. Three times I was beaten with rods. Once I received a stoning. Three times I was shipwrecked; for a night and a day I was adrift at sea; on frequent journeys, in danger from rivers, danger from bandits, danger from my own people, danger from Gentiles, danger in the city, danger in the wilderness, danger at sea, danger from false brothers and sisters; in toil and hardship, through many a sleepless night, hungry and thirsty, often without food, cold and naked. And, besides other things, I am under daily pressure because of my anxiety for all the churches. Who is weak, and I am not weak? Who is made to stumble, and I am not indignant? (NRSV)

To be conformed like him in his death does not likely mean that Paul is expecting to be crucified like Christ was. His Roman citizenship precluded this. The verb *synmorphizomenos* is only found here in the New Testament. The present tense emphasizes the ongoing process of being conformed to his likeness. Paul is probably thinking of the life-cycle of human mortality and the toll that ministry exacts on this life-cycle. He spells this out in 2 Cor 4:9–11: "Persecuted, but not forsaken; struck down, but not destroyed; always carrying in this body the death of Jesus, so that the life of Jesus may also be made visible in our bodies. For while we live, we are always being given up to death for Jesus' sake, so that the life of Jesus may be made visible in our mortal flesh" (NRSV).

Paul's final statement is equally difficult to unpack. Most translate: "If somehow I may attain to the resurrection of the dead." Some translate "raised from death." However, the Greek *nekrōn* is plural. "From among the dead" is the sense. It certainly is not that Paul is doubting that he will be among those experiencing resurrection at Christ's return. All the dead will be raised. The unbeliever will be raised to face judgment "on the day when, according to [Paul's] gospel, God, through Jesus Christ, will judge the secret thoughts of all" (Rom 2:16). The believer will be raised to join the living at which point all will be transfigured: "In a moment, in the twinkling of an eye, at the last trumpet. For the trumpet will sound, and the dead will be raised imperishable, and we will be changed" (1 Cor 15:52). It could be an expression of humility. Paul may be hoping that resurrection and transformation are in his future but not wanting to presume. This needs to be balanced with texts like 2 Cor 5:10, where Paul states: "We must all appear before the judgment seat of Christ," which presumes resurrection.

Paul continues with a disclaimer. **Not that I have already attained it or have already reached the goal** (*teteleiōmai*). The goal is commonly understood to be spiritual perfection. Paul may have been **blameless** in terms of Jewish legal righteousness. However, that is not the perfection in view here. Sanctification is the theological term in view—to be conformed to the likeness of Christ. Although Wesleyan theology posits that total sanctification is attainable in this life, Paul's disclaimer suggests otherwise.[6] He may not yet possess it in full. However, he **pursues it so as to take hold of** it. Paul likens the process of sanctification to that of an Olympic runner in the familiar Greek foot-race. There was a stadium with tiers of seats, which looked down on a course that was about 607 feet in length. Near the entrance to the course the contestants, stripped for the race and were assigned their places on a stone threshold. The blocks of stone contained grooves to give the sprinter's feet a firm hold for a quick take-off. The contestants stood with their body bent forward and one hand lightly touching the threshold. At the signal they lept forward.

What goes through the mind of the runner at this time? For Paul it involves, first of all, to **pursue** it with the effort needed **to take hold of it**. While some translate the Greek "I press on," the term *diōkō* means "to pursue with single-minded concentration." Nothing is permitted to divert the runner from his or her course (LSJ). Second, **I forget what lies behind me**. One of the worst mistakes that a runner can make is to get distracted by how the competition is doing behind him or her. This is also one of the mistakes we can make in the Christian life. We can get distracted by how we are doing in comparison with others. Third, **I strain forward to take hold of what lies ahead**. This is a picture of a runner straining every nerve and muscle toward the goal and with hand stretched out as if to grasp it. Fourth, Paul **pursues the goal.** In ancient Greece the goal or mark was a pillar at the end of the track, which the runners riveted their eyes on throughout the race. For the Christian, the goal we are to fix our eyes on is Christ himself. Heb 12:1–2 expresses the idea well: "Let us lay aside every weight and the

6. According to Louw and Nida, it is important that *teleioō* be understood in the sense of a functional stage of religious attainment (L&N 53.50). For an alternative interpretation, see L&N 68.31. For the Wesleyan perspective, see Wesley 1738: 124–26.

sin that clings so closely, and let us run with perseverance the race that is set before us, looking to Jesus the pioneer and perfecter of our faith" (NRSV). Fifth, Paul aims to cross the finish line and **receive the prize.** The runner never forgets the prize. For the Greek runner it was a wreath of olive leaves intertwined to form a circle or a horseshoe. The judges of the Olympic games would make the wreaths and crown the winner.[7] All the winners would be honored at a lavish celebration and their name memorialized for future generations.[8] For the believer, the **prize** is **God's heavenly calling in Christ Jesus** (*tēs anō klēseōs*): "To the one who is victorious, I [Christ] will grant the right to sit with me on my throne just as I overcame and sat down with my Father on his throne" (Rev 3:21).

Fusing the Horizons: Pressing Toward the Goal

Paul states that he presses with all his might toward the finish line so as to cross and receive his heavenly prize. It is very easy in our culture to let the claims of family, friends, job, school, social media, and cell phones to encroach on and even replace Christ's claim on our lives. Like the Olympic footrace, pressing towards God's finish line involves hard work and personal discipline. It requires a commitment of our time as well as a commitment of our heart. As the author of Hebrews states: We "fix our eyes on Jesus, the author and perfector of our faith, who for the joy set before him endured the cross, scorning its shame, and sat down at the right hand of the throne of God" (Heb 12:2).

The Greek runner ran in such a way as to cross the finish line and receive his prize. "The upward call" for the runner was the moment when they were

---

7. Pausanias, *Descr.* 5.7.7. One event that was not in the ancient Olympic Games was the marathon. What is called a marathon today gets its name from the 140 mile distance covered by the runner Pheidippides over the course of three to four days from Athens to Sparta. He ran to get the help of the Spartans against the attack of the Persian army in the Battle of Marathon in 490 BC. See Herodotus, *The Greco-Persian Wars.* Legend has it that Pheidippides then ran the 25 miles (40 km) from Marathon to Athens to announce their victory over the Persians. See Plutarch, *Moralia* 347C-D. In 1896 the first modern-day marathon was run. To honor the history of Greek running, Greece chose a course that mimicked the route run by Pheidippides. The race course covered 24.85 miles (40 km) The distance eventually became fixed at 26 miles (42.195 km).

8. The victorious athletes in the Olympic games were honored and praised at a grand celebration. Their deeds were heralded and chronicled so that future generations would appreciate their accomplishments. See Timaeus, *The Histories of Rome.* Also Brown 1958.

summoned to approach an elevated platform where the judge was waiting to give him the prize of being crowned with an olive wreath. For the Christian, it is the moment when we cross the finish line and hear the words: "Good and faithful servant . . . come and share your master's happiness" (Matt 25:23 (NIV).

Keeping in Step: 3:15—4:1

[15]Therefore let us who are "mature" be of the same mind. If you think differently, God will also reveal this to you. [16]However, let us keep in step with what we have already attained. [17]Continue imitating me, dear friends, and focus on those who live according to the example you have in us. [18]For many live as enemies of Christ's cross. I have often told you about them and now tell you again with weeping. [19]Their end is destruction. Their god is their appetite. They take pride in what they should be ashamed of. They focus on earthly things. [20]Instead our citizenship is in heaven from which we receive a Savior, the Lord Jesus Christ, who will transform our humble body to be conformed to his glorious body. [21]by the powerful work of him who will submit everything to him. [4:1]So dear friends, my beloved whom I long for, my joy and crown, continue to stand firm in the Lord, beloved.

Paul goes on to deal with those at Philippi who **think differently** from what he has taught due to the influence of outsiders that he calls **enemies of Christ's cross** (v. 18). They are not the model to follow. This is not hypothetical. **If you think differently** is a first-class conditional that assumes fact (*ei* + the indicative; BDF #372). The intruders have caused some at Philippi to change their thinking. Paul's response is to remind the church of the appropriate spiritual models. He has already set before them the model of Christ (2:5–11). However, if more is needed, Paul tells them to:

- Continue down the path that they have been on (v. 16)
- Continue imitating Paul's example (v. 17a)
- Focus on those who follow Paul's example (v. 17b)

As for the rest, Paul tells them to trust **God will reveal this to** them.

Paul returns to the importance of unity: **Be of the same mind**. Unity is a mark of the **mature** person(v. 15). Although *hosoi teleioi* is commonly translated "those who are perfect," the Greek term here has more to do with maturity (Anlex [2]). The *hosoi teleioi* are those who have a mature spiritual understanding. They have become spiritual adults as opposed to infants or children in their thinking (cf. 1 Cor 2:6). To **be of the same mind** requires that the Philippians **keep in step with** the level of understanding they **have already attained** (v. 16). The Greek *phthanō* ("attain") means to overtake others (LSJ). The previous picture of a long-distance runner may be in view. The Philippians are ahead of the pack. To maintain their position, they must **keep in step** (*stoichein*) so as not to fall behind. The picture is to walk in step with others much as members of a marching band do (L&N).

Paul also commands them to **continue imitating** him (v. 17). This can sound a bit arrogant. However, Paul's ministry smacks of anything but arrogance. As he has already said, he counted all his religious accomplishments as a loss. They have been replaced in the asset column with the ministerial hardships and suffering that Christ also endured. 1 Cor 4:11–13 is representative: "To the present hour we are hungry and thirsty, we are poorly clothed and beaten and homeless, and we grow weary from the work of our own hands. When reviled, we bless; when persecuted, we endure; when slandered, we speak kindly. We have become like the rubbish of the world, the dregs of all things, to this very day" (NRSV).

Since Paul is not physically accessible at the time of writing, he tells the church to seek out others whose conduct follows his pattern: **Those who live according to the example you have in us.** "**Example**" translates the Greek *typos*, which refers to the impression left behind by a blow (Anlex). The conduct of those who follow Paul make an indelible impression on others. As is common in Paul's letters, the Christian life is described as a "walk" (*peripateō*). The Philippians' job is to "walk the walk" of the spiritually mature. To do this requires keeping a "close eye on" their behavior. They are to **focus** on the spiritually mature (*skopeite*; L&N). Paul is not calling for casual observation but a careful inspection of the model and **example** that the church has in Paul and his colleagues (**in us**; Anlex).

By contrast the intruders at Philippi **live as enemies of Christ's cross.** Paul had **often told** them this and **now tells** them **again with weeping** (v. 18). Paul's description of these intruders makes identification difficult. True, they are Paul's enemies but more importantly they are **enemies of Christ's cross.** This suggests that the intruders are Jewish proselytizing unbelievers, who can't accept a crucified Messiah. In 1 Cor 1:23 Paul states: "We proclaim Christ crucified, a stumbling block to Jews and foolishness to Gentiles." The Greek term for the NRSV "stumbling block" is *skandalon*, meaning "offensive," "scandalous" (L&N). "Christ crucified" didn't fit Jewish expectation of a Messiah who would come as a conqueror of their Roman captors. A crucified Messiah is an oxymoron for an orthodox Jew. It is what makes Jewish conversions so difficult. It required Christ's intervention as Paul headed to Damascus with authoritative letters from the chief priests to arrest Christ followers (Acts 9:1–21).

Paul goes further to state: **Their end is destruction; their god is their appetite; they take pride in what they should be ashamed of.** (v. 19). Although this sounds a bit harsh coming from a Jewish rabbi and Pharisee, the fact is that destruction will be their end, if they persist in their rejection of the crucified Christ. Paul doesn't say this lightly. He reminds the church that he tells them this **with weeping.** Although some translate the Greek *klaiōn* "with tears," the emotion is much stronger: "to "weep," "wail," "lament" (LSJ). By **destruction** Paul may not be thinking of eternal damnation but rather "their utter ruin" or "loss" (L&N). The path that these Jewish proselytizers are currently on will not end in their success but their ruin. Paul states in 2 Cor 2:15–16:

> "For we are the aroma of Christ to God among those who are being saved and among those who are perishing; to the one a fragrance from death to death, to the other a fragrance from life to life" (NRSV).

Their god is their appetite at face value is a good description of Greek orgies. Most, therefore, translate the Greek *koilia* as "their god is their belly" (NRSV).[9] Perhaps Paul has in mind the care with which orthodox Jews observed Jewish dietary laws and regulations. Alternatively, *koilia* can refer to a person's appetites: "For such people do not serve our Lord Christ, but their own *appetites*, and by smooth talk and flattery they deceive the hearts of the simple-minded" (Rom 16:18). **They take pride in what they should be ashamed of** is probably referring to the Jewish covenantal rite of circumcision. Circumcision was the identity marker for belonging to God's covenantal people. Paul now asserts that Christ has replaced circumcision as the identity marker. Circumcision now belongs to the realm of **earthly things.**

9. Compare Moiser 1997: 365–66 on the meaning of *koilia*. See Still 2011: 422–28 for an overview of recent scholarly literature.

Paul by contrast focuses the church's need to look upward ("heavenly") versus downward ("earthly"). The Jewish intruders' minds are set on **earthly things** so that they have lost any ability to look upward (cf. Col 3:2). **Our citizenship is in heaven** is unique to this letter (v. 20). Paul's location in a Roman prison likely influenced his choice of words. Roman citizenship was highly prized in Paul's day. Some gained it through military service. Others bought citizenship. The Roman tribune in Jerusalem said: "It cost me a large sum of money to get my citizenship" (Acts 22:28). Still others inherited it. Paul responded: "But I was born a citizen" (Acts 22:28). What Christians should value is not their earthly citizenship but their heavenly one.

Verses 20–21 are packed with theology that Paul treats at much greater length elsewhere. **From which** [heaven] **we receive a Savior, the Lord Jesus Christ** is the focus of 1–2 Thessalonians.[10] Paul states: "For the Lord himself shall descend from heaven with a shout, with the voice of the archangel" (1 Thess 4:16; cf. 1 Thess 1:10). Paul's reference to receiving **a Savior** from heaven suggests the rescue campaign found in 2 Thess 1:7–8: "to give relief to the afflicted as well as to us, when the Lord Jesus is revealed from heaven with his mighty angels in flaming fire, inflicting vengeance on those who do not know God and on those who do not obey the Gospel of our Lord Jesus." Paul states that this heavenly redeemer will **transform our humble body to be conformed to his glorious body.**[11]

There is no mention of resurrecting the dead in Christ. Paul's focus is on those who are alive, by reminding them of their theological hope. Although they face persecution and suffering from strong opponents, **the Lord Jesus Christ** will not only descend with his heavenly army to rescue them, but will also **transform** their earthly body into one that is free from all mortal ills: "For our dying bodies must be transformed into bodies that will never die; our mortal bodies must be transformed into immortal bodies" (1 Cor 15:53 NLT). **Conformed to** recalls Phil 2:6, where Christ's "divine" *morphē* ("form") took on an earthly, mortal *morphē* ("form") that suffered and experienced death. His mortal "form" was **transformed** into an immortal "form." So we too experience the mortal becoming immortal, which Paul describes as **conformed to** [Christ's] **glorious body.** This is accomplished **by the powerful work of him who will submit everything to him** (v. 21). **The powerful work of him** is God, **who will submit everything**

10. See Meeks 1991: 329–36 on "the man from heaven."
11. See Doble 2003: 3–27 regarding the question of transformation.

to him, that is, to Christ. **Power** (*energeian*) in the New Testament refers to the result of divine activity (Anlex). It is the term used of the power to work miracles (1 Cor 12:6, 10). God's power will effect the **submission** of **everything to him.** The term "submission" (*hypotaxai*) has a different nuance than that of "obedience" (*hypakoē*). "Submission" is a voluntary waiving of one's prerogative to another (Anlex "with a component of voluntary submission"). Paul already referenced this submission in chapter 2:10–11: "At the name of Jesus each and every knee will bow, in heaven and on earth and under the earth, and every tongue will publicly acknowledge that Jesus Christ is Lord, to the glory of God the Father."

Paul lets out all the stops in his final call for the church to **continue to stand firm in the Lord.** The present tense of the verb *stēkete* emphasizes the need to keep doing what they have been doing. The piling up of words of endearment stresses his deep affection for the Philippians. Twice he calls them **my beloved** (4:1). He **longs for** them, the word *epitpothētoi* referring to a yearning affection (L&N). They are his **joy and crown.** The grammar points to a single unit. The genitive *mou* ("my") governs both nouns, which are connected by **and** (*kai*).[12] The church is not "*my* joy and *my* crown," but "*my* joy-and-crown."[13] The **crown** (*stephanos*) would be the laurel wreath placed on the head of the winner of an athletic event (LSJ).

12. Greenlee 1986: 23.

13. See Holloway 2001 on consolation in Philippians and Paul's rhetorical strategy.

Philippians 4

A Call for Unity Among the Leadership: 4:2-3

> [2]I ask Euodia and I ask Syntyche to be of the same mind in the Lord. [3]I also ask you, my loyal companion, to help them. For they struggled beside me in the gospel work along with Clement and the rest of my co-workers, whose names are in the book of life.

The term *parakalō* signals a transition in Paul's letters:[1] **I ask** (*parakalō*) **Euodia and I ask** (*parakalō*) **Syntyche to be of the same mind in the Lord**. The double *parakalō* is rare. Paul is addressing Euodia and Syntyche not as a team but as individuals with differing opinions. It is also very rare for Paul to name names in his letters. In part, the public nature of his letters precluded naming names. Letters were written to be read out loud and concerned matters that affected the whole church. In Col 4:16, Paul states: "When this letter has been read among you, have it read also in the church of the Laodiceans; and see that you also read the letter from Laodicea."[2] When Paul does mention someone by name it is with decided intentionality. For him to do so here is indicative of the stature of these two women within the community of faith. Euodia's and Syntyche's differences were not of a petty or personal nature. Paul talks of conflict in the church and exhorts the Philippians to stand firm in one spirit (1:27), to strive side-by-side as one person for the gospel faith (1:27), not to be intimidated by their opponents (1:28), and to be of the same mind (2:2, 5; 3:15). The same language is used of Euodia and Syntyche. They too are called **to be of the same mind in the Lord,** having **struggled beside** Paul **in the gospel work** (vv. 2-3). Their role so clearly involved a leadership role that their disagreement was affecting the church's ability to face outside opposition with a

1. See Doty 1973: 34.
2. Idem: 45-46.

86

united front. The letter is addressed to **the overseers and deacons who live in Philippi.** Euodia and Syntyche could well have been part of this group of leaders.

Paul's initial evangelistic foray in Philippi took place among a group of Jewish women during Sabbath prayers (Acts 16:13–15). Some, such as Euodia and Syntyche, then partnered with Paul in preaching the gospel as well as in leading the congregation. Paul states that they **struggled beside me in the gospel work.** The term **struggled beside me** (a word for hand-to-hand combat) suggests that they along with Paul faced strong opposition during their evangelistic work (*synēthlēsan* L&N: "to toil together with someone in a struggle, implying opposition").

Paul calls upon **And you loyal companion** (*kai se gnēsie syzyge,*), to help these women. The verb is different. His request of Euodia and Syntyche is *parakalō*, which is used in Greco-Roman culture of a request by someone who has the authority to command but waives it in a specific situation.[3] Here Paul uses the culturally routine "I ask" (*erōtaō* L&N). There is no other mention of this individual in the New Testament and this is the only place Paul addresses a co-worker directly in a letter. There is some debate about to whom Paul is referring. Some translate the Greek *syzyge* as a personal name (Syzyge). However no such Greek name exists. *Syzyge* means "to be yoked together" and was a familiar farming term for the importance of the equal yoking of animals who are tilling the soil. Josephus states: "You are to plough your land with oxen, and not to oblige other animals to come under the same yoke with them, but to till your land with those beasts that are of the same kind with each other."[4] The Greek term translated **loyal** (*hyēsie*) indicates that this was a Christian who was much valued by Paul as a co-worker in the apostolic mission.

Clement and the rest of my co-workers were also part of the evangelistic group. There is no other mention of Clement elsewhere in the New Testament. However, Irenaeus and Tertullian connect him with the late-first-century Roman bishop who wrote a letter to the Corinthian church (1 Clement). He is considered to be one of three chief apostolic fathers (along with Polycarp and Ignatius of Antioch).[5]

---

3. For a detailed analysis of the formulaic features of the Hellenistic letter, see White 1971.

4. Josephus, *Ant.* 4.228.

5. See Cross 2005.

A Call For Ethical Conduct: 4:4–9

> [4]Continue to rejoice in the Lord always. Again I say rejoice. [5]Let your restraint be known to all people. The Lord is near. [6]Stop being anxious for anything but in everything with prayer and petition with thanksgiving, let your requests be made known to God. [7]God's peace, which surpasses all understanding, will guard your hearts and minds in Christ Jesus. [8]Finally, brothers and sisters, whatever is true, honorable, righteous, pure, admirable, praiseworthy and virtuous, keep dwelling on such things. [9]And that which you learned, received, and have seen in me, continue to do. God's peace will be with you all.

It is common for Paul to include a section of paraenesis, where he calls the reader(s) to live a moral life. A paraenetic section is unique to Paul as a first-century letter writer. It is commonly placed before the closing section of the letter.[6] Paraenesis can also be found in the body closing itself. Similar to the letter form of his day, Paul includes a body closing section, where there is (1) a closing reference to writing ("I Paul am writing . . ."), (2) expressions urging responsibility, and (3) a notification of an upcoming visit. Paul adds an expression of confidence ("I'm glad that I can have complete confidence in you"; 2 Cor 7:16) but omits the usual request for a letter.

Paul puts notification of an upcoming visit much earlier in Philippians and of more length than is common (2:19–30). Notification of an upcoming visit is a central part of the first-century letter. However, it usually appears in the closing section of the letter's main body just prior to final greetings and farewell. That Paul moved notification of travel plans to an earlier point in the letter indicates concern. The typical newsy information is missing. His typical expressions urging responsible action occur there as well. Paul shows great concern about the welcome that Epaphroditus and Timothy will receive: "Welcome him then in the Lord with all joy . . ." (2:29).

His reason for writing follows his disclosure of travel plans: **For me to write these things to you is not bothersome but a way to keep you on firm footing** (3:1). Some argue that this structural separation points to multiple letters. However, 1 and 2 Corinthians also include travel plans and a reference to writing earlier in the letter. This occurs when the travel plans serve a strategic function in addressing problems. In the case of 1 Corinthians, Paul states in chapter 4 that he will be coming soon and discipline those who say that he has abandoned them. In 2 Corinthians, news

---

6. White 1986: 220.

of travel plans occur in chapter 7 in response to Titus's return with news of the church.

Paul begins by issuing five commands:

- Continue to rejoice in the Lord
- Let your restraint be known to all
- Stop being anxious for anything
- Keep dwelling on admirable behavior
- Continue to follow my example

Continue to rejoice in the Lord always. Again I say rejoice advances the major theme of "joy" and "rejoicing" in the letter (v. 4).[7] His close relationship with the Philippian church explains his joy, when recalling this relationship. It may appear odd that Paul adds **again I say rejoice.** However, Paul commanded earlier: **Now for the rest, my brothers and sisters, continue to rejoice in the Lord** (3:1). **Again I say rejoice** is Paul acknowledging that he already issued this command. Yet, it does deserve repeating. He uses the present tense, acknowledging that they have been rejoicing in the past and now, when facing persecution and opposition, they especially need to continue doing so.

Let your restraint be known to all people (v. 5). While retaliation might be the normal response to persecution, Paul commands **restraint.** Even a proportionate response is discouraged. Although some translations have: "Let your gentleness (or 'meekness') be known to all," the sense is forbearance or **restraint** (*epieikeis*). Paul is not advocating gentleness in the face of persecution, but rather **restraint.** Paul had just referred to their heavenly citizenship, Christ the Lord as their returning Savior, and the glorious transformation of their bodies (v. 20). **The Lord is near** (v. 5). Hence they can show **restraint** in their response (cf. Act 24:4).[8] Paul's command: **Stop being anxious for anything,** is *mē* + the present imperative, indicating that the Philippians were expressing anxiety and needed to stop doing so. Paul's command is a repetition of Jesus's command to his disciples. In Matt 6:25, 34 Jesus tells his disciples: "Therefore I tell you, *stop* worrying about your life, what you will eat or what you will drink, or about your body, what you will wear. Is not life more than food, and the body more than clothing? . . . So do not *start* worrying again about tomorrow (*me* +

---

7. Phil 1:4, 18, 25; 2:2, 17 (4x), 18, 28, 29; 3:1; 4:1, 4, 10.

8. See Herbert Preisker, "ἐπιεικεῖς" *TDNT* 2:590.

the aorist imperative), for tomorrow will bring worries of its own. Today's trouble is enough for today.

Anxiety about one's current or future circumstances is common to all of us. Paul's solution is prayer: **Let your requests be made known to God** (v. 6). The Greek *deēsis* ("request") is occasionally used by Paul, when making a request of his readers. However, his usual term is *parakalō*, which is used in Greco-Roman culture of a request by someone who has the authority to command. *Deēsis*, on the other hand, is typically used between equals.[9] However, when used of a request of God, it carries a nuance of urgency based on presumed need. An angel tells Zechariah, "Do not be afraid" for "God has heard your request" (*deēsis*; Luke 1:13).

Such a request is to be made **with thanksgiving.** Thanksgiving assumes that God will respond and hence they should pray with gratitude. There is no place for anxiety in any circumstance. **Everything** is to be lifted up in prayer.

Paul concludes with the assurance that **God's peace, which surpasses all understanding, will guard your hearts and minds in Christ Jesus** (v. 7). Philippi in Paul's time housed a Roman garrison.[10] Thus the metaphor would have been easily understood and appreciated by the Philippian Christians who read it. God's peace, like a garrison of soldiers, will keep guard over our thoughts and feelings so that they will be as safe against the assaults of worry and fear as any fortress.

God's peace will guard seems at first sight like a contradiction. However, **guard** has the sense here of protection from harm. Hence, the idea of God guarding our **hearts and minds** from anxious thoughts fits the context. God's peace **surpasses all understanding.** The human response to danger is one of fight or flight. God's protection is 24-7. He "neither slumbers nor sleeps" (Ps 121:4).

Finally, Paul states, **whatever is true, honorable, just, pure, admirable, praiseworthy and virtuous, keep dwelling on such things. Keep dwelling on** (*logizomai*) as a subjective act of thought means "to have in mind," "ponder," "think about" (L&N). The present tense indicates the need to keep on thinking about and pondering the virtues Paul lists. The virtues Paul lists are common in both Platonic and Aristotelian ethics. His list recalls the moral philosophers of his day, who taught by reciting catalogues of virtues and vices. **True and honorable** conduct were prized as both Greek

9. White 1971: 90–93.
10. Bakirtzis 1998: 49–50.

and Roman virtues. **Just and pure** are two sides of the same coin. Right living and pure motives are key moral virtues in Paul's letters. The Greek word translated **admirable** refers to what is pleasing and lovely (Anlex). That which is pleasing and lovely is **praiseworthy** (Anlex). The final adjective **virtuous** (*aretē*) denotes moral excellence and outstanding goodness (L&N). As Aristotle says: "At the right times, about the right things, towards the right people, for the right end, and in the right way."[11] The fact that many of the words in Paul's list are found only here in the New Testament suggests that Paul has taken over these "virtues," from popular moral philosophy familiar to his contemporaries.

Paul is not telling them to do what he hasn't done himself. They **learned, received and have seen** all these virtues in Paul's own teaching and conduct. This is why Paul earlier commanded them to **keep imitating** him (3:17; cf. 1 Cor 4:15). He taught not only by word but also by living example. They saw a pattern of the Christian life in him (when present) and heard about him (when he was absent). Finally, not only will God's peace guard their hearts and minds, but this very **God of peace will be with** them **all. For we are the temple of the living God.** As God said: "I will live in them and walk among them and I will be their God and they will be my people" (2 Cor 6:16).

A *Thankyou Note: 4:10–20*

> [10]I greatly rejoiced in the Lord that now at last you have revived you concern for me. Indeed, you were concerned but had no opportunity to show it. [11]Not that I am talking about being in need. For I learned to be content with whatever I have. [12]I know what it is to have little and I know what it is to have much. In each and every situation, I have learned the secret of being well-fed or of going hungry and of having plenty or of being in need. [13]I can do all things through him who empowers me .[14]Even so, you Philippians did well by sharing with me in my suffering. [15]For you know that in the early days of the Gospel, after I left Macedonia, no church shared with me in giving and receiving except you alone. [16]Even when I was in Thessalonica, you sent me help for my needs more than once. [17]Not that I seek the gift but I seek the fruit which abounds for you. [18]I have been paid in full and have more than enough. I am fully satisfied now that I have received from Epaphroditus the gifts you sent. They are a fragrant offering, a sacrifice

11. Aristotle, *Eth. nic.* 124.

> acceptable and pleasing to God. [19]My God will fully satisfy every
> need of yours according to his riches in glory in Christ Jesus. [20]To
> our God and Father be glory forever and ever. Amen.

Once again Paul returns to the theme of rejoicing. This time he rejoices over the gifts that the Philippians sent with Epaphroditus to meet his needs (v. 18). Thankfulness for a church's support does not appear elsewhere in Paul's letters. In the letters of the day, a statement of thanks appears right after the letter opening. It does as well in Philippians. However, it is the typical thanks Paul gives to God for a church's continuing faith but not for their financial support. However, this should not surprise, since Paul's relationship with the Philippian church was special. The Philippians were Paul's **beloved, whom he longed for** with all the depth of his being (1:8). They were his pride and joy (4:1).

The fact that it has been quite some time since the church provided financial help (*ēdē pote* "now at last"), supports a late date and Roman location for Paul's letter. His founding visit is dated c. AD 50. While he was in Corinth (c. AD 53), he employed his trade (along with Priscilla and Aquila) as a tentmaker (using goathair) to support himself rather than depending on church support (Acts 18:3). When he writes to the Corinthian church from Ephesus in c. AD 54 and again in Macedonia in c. AD 57, he notes that the Macedonian churches gave to the collection for the Jerusalem church despite their "severe poverty" (*bathous ptōcheia*; 2 Cor 8:1–5). A Roman imprisonment c. AD 62 would provide ample time for the Philippians to recoup their losses and be able to provide support **now at last**. Also, the fact that Paul states that they **were concerned but had no opportunity to show it** suggests a later date as does the graphic term **revived**, which is used of plants shooting up, becoming green and flourishing again (v. 10; Anlex).

In verses 11–13 Paul provides us with a theology of Christian contentment. The Greek term for contentment (*autarkēs*) in Cynic and Stoic philosophy refers to self-sufficiency as opposed to dependence on others.[12] Paul differed from Cynic and Stoic understanding in a significant respect. He pursued God-dependency rather than self-sufficiency. The generous giver like the farmer is dependent from start to finish on God (2 Cor 9:10). Contentment is not instantaneous. Paul **learned to be content with whatever** he had (v. 11). For him the Greek term *autarkēs* carries the idea of contentment regardless of one's circumstances.

---

12. Gerhard Kittel, "αὐτάρκεια," *TDNT* 1:466–67.

Regardless of his circumstances, Paul **learned the secret** of **being well-fed or of going hungry and of having plenty or of being in need. Secret** (*memyēmai*) is a technical term for initiation into the sacred mystery religions.[13] This is its only occurrence in the New Testament. The passive (as here) means to learn the secrets of that religion (LSJ). The **secret** for Paul was: **I can do all things through him who strengthens me** (v. 13). Regardless of what Paul faced he was strong (*ischyō*). The Greek term *ischyō*, commonly understood as physically "strong," is used here of having the capacity to face whatever is thrown one's way (L&N). This capacity is not a matter of pulling oneself up by one's bootstraps, that is, to improve one's situation through hard work and self-determination. That is Stoic philosophy. The capacity that Paul has in mind comes from God. God is he who "empowers" (*endyamounti* L&N).

Even so, Paul states, **you Philippians did well by sharing with me in my suffering** (*thlipsis* v. 14). Some translate *thlipsis* as "trouble" or "hardship." However, *thlipsis* is a term Paul uses exclusively for Christian suffering. He is no longer talking about the hardship of being hungry. The account in Acts amply demonstrates the persecution that Paul faced. Indeed, Paul's sufferings exceeded those of other Christians. The Lord assured Ananias that Paul's conversion was genuine: "Go, for he is an instrument whom I have chosen to bring my name before Gentiles and kings and before the people of Israel. I myself will show him how much he must suffer for the sake of my name" (Acts 9:15–16).

References to *thlipsis* the New Testament are common.[14] Those who experience *thlipsis* are followers of Christ.[15] Suffering is necessary.[16] Paul tells the Thessalonican church that he sent Timothy to them "so that no one would be shaken by these persecutions (*tais thlipsesin tautais*). Indeed, you yourselves know that this is what we are destined for (*eis touto keimetha*). In fact, when we were with you, we told you beforehand that we were to suffer persecution and so it turned out, as you know" (1 Thess 3:3–4).

Paul reminds the Philippians **that in the early days of the gospel after I left Macedonia, no church shared with me in giving and receiving except you alone** (v. 15). This is information that we do not find in Acts or

---

13. Günther Bornkamm, "μεμύημαι," *TDNT* 4:827.

14. *Thlipsis* is used 45 times in the New Testament of which 22 are found in Paul.

15. See, for example, Mark 4:17; Acts 11:19; Rom 5:3; 2 Cor 1:4; 1 Thess 1:6; 3:7; 2 Thess 1:4; Heb 10:33; Rev 1:9.

16. Cf. John 16:33: "In the world you have suffering" (*en tō kosmō thlipsin echete*).

elsewhere in Paul's letters. Paul clarifies: **Even when I was in Thessalonica, you sent me help for my needs more than once** (v. 16). Although some translations have the Philippians sending Paul supplies "once and twice," the Greek phrase is idiomatic for more than once (L&N).[17] By contrast, Paul tells the Corinthians that, although he could expect support as a gospel "laborer," he chose not to do so. Instead his reward was "that in my proclamation I may make the gospel free of charge, so as not to make full use of my rights in the gospel" (1 Cor 9:14–18). His refusal was so that no one could claim that he preached for the money. This distinguished him (and his co-workers) from the many itinerant speakers and preachers of the day who expected to receive support (1 Cor 2:1, 4):

> When I came to you, brothers and sisters, I did not come proclaiming the mystery of God to you in lofty words or wisdom. For I decided to know nothing among you except Jesus Christ and him crucified. And I came to you in weakness and in fear and in much trembling. My speech and my proclamation were not with plausible words of wisdom but with a demonstration of the Spirit and of power, so that your faith might rest not on human wisdom but on the power of God.

Although Paul appreciates their support of his needs, what he emphasizes is the spiritual aspect of their giving: **Not that I seek the gift but I seek the fruit which abounds for you** (v. 17). **Fruit** is a sign of health. A healthy tree produces fruit. The spiritual health of a Christian is evidenced by the fruit that he or she produces. In turn, Paul expects the Philippians to receive God blessings because of the support which they have given him: **My God will fully satisfy every need of yours according to his riches in glory in Christ Jesus** (v. 19). A similar idea is found with reference to the Jerusalem collection. The Corinthians' gift will meet the need of the Jerusalem church and area churches. This, in turn, will result in God enriching them "in every way" (2 Cor 9:11) with the churches "many thanksgivings" and prayers for them (9:12).

However, now Paul states: **I have been paid in full and have more than enough. I am fully satisfied now.** Their gift is **a fragrant offering, a sacrifice acceptable and pleasing to God** (v. 18). Paul's language is familiar

---

17. The Philippians' special relationship to Paul is well attested throughout the letter. Paul uses strong language, when describing his feelings toward the church: "You are very dear to my heart" (1:8); "I long for all of you with the affection of Christ Jesus himself" (1:9).

to both Greeks and Jews. Greco-Roman cities had their temples and sacrifices, and the first converts at Philippi were Jewish women (Acts 16). **Acceptable and pleasing to God** recalls Old Testament sacrificial stipulations. An offering to God first appears, when Cain brought an offering to the Lord from the fruit of the ground and Abel brought one from his flock (Gen 4:3–5). It was the burning of the offering that made it a pleasing aroma to the Lord. The first mention of God smelling the aroma of a burnt offering is when Noah offered a burnt offering of clean animals and birds, after leaving the ark. It was a "pleasing aroma" to God (Gen 8:21). What makes the sacrifice a pleasing aroma is not the smell but what the smell represents. This is clear from Paul calling Christ's death on the cross for us "a fragrant offering and sacrifice to God" (Eph 5:2). Mention of the Philippians' fragrant gift leads Paul to end with a doxology: "To our God and Father be glory forever and ever, Amen" (v. 20).

Fusing the Horizons: The Blessings of Giving

Motivating Christians and congregations not only to give but to be fiscally responsible in their giving is a difficult enterprise even in the best of circumstances. The needs are seemingly endless and there are so many competing voices that the average Christian is stymied by the constant and often relentless pursuit of those asking for money. The responsible fundraiser is frequently in no less of a quandary as they face the consumerism mentality of our global society. Books on how to corner the market are on the increase. Sophisticated marketing strategies abound. Then there are those who make a bad name for fundraisers everywhere by resorting to threats (e.g., to go without food until a certain dollar figure is met), sensationalism (e.g., pictures of children with severe deformities) and even warnings of impending doom for the organization, if funds are not immediately forthcoming.

In the final analysis, the key to giving lies in the attitude of the heart. It must be a "willing" gift: "If the willingness is there, then the gift is acceptable" (2 Cor 8:12). It is not the amount that counts with God. If a readiness to give is present, then the gift is gladly received, whether it be large or small. Some years ago a woman was preparing a box to be sent to some missionaries in India. A child gave her a penny which she used to purchase a tract for the box. Eventually this tract reached a Burmese chief and was used to lead him to Christ. The chief told the story of his conversion to his friends, many of whom believed. Eventually a church was established and over 1,500 people were converted to Christianity. The lesson is plain: No gift willingly given is too small for God to use.[18]

William Barclay correctly observes that Christ's sacrifice did not begin on the cross, nor even at birth. It began in heaven, when he laid aside his glory and consented to come to earth.[19] Christ did this "so that in him we might become the righteousness of God" (2 Cor 5:21). To put it another way, Christ went from riches to rags, so that we might go from rags to riches. What are these riches? Although Paul talked earlier about the Philippians' rich produce of spiritual fruit (1:11), it is equally likely that he is also thinking of the riches of salvation.

Final Greetings: 4:21–23

> [21]Greet all God's people in Christ Jesus. The brothers and sisters who are with me send greetings. [22]All God's people here send you greetings, especially those who belong to Caesar's household. [23]The grace of the Lord Jesus Christ be with your spirit.

"Greet so and so" is the typical way we close our letters today. It was the same in Paul's day. The greeting had a twofold purpose in the Hellenistic letter. It was used to mark the transition from the body of the letter to its close. It also served to strengthen the relationship between the writer and the reader(s).

The greetings in Philippians are very brief and general. However, it is important not to read too much into the fact that Paul does not give specific greetings. To churches that he knew well, he tended to conclude with the most general of greetings. It is to churches that he did not know personally, such as the churches at Rome and Colossae, that he sent and solicited detailed greetings (Rom 16:1–23; Col 4:7–15). This is understandable. To the familiar church there would be a tendency to keep it brief and general so as to not give offense to anyone whose name might be left off the list. To the unfamiliar church, however, specific greetings would be an important bridging device.

18. Belleville 1996: 218–24.
19. Barclay 1954: 229.

Philippians is distinctive in the greeting **especially** from **those who belong to Caesar's household.** As his trial begins ("In my defense" 1:7), Paul would be moved to a place of confinement. His earlier reference to the **Praetorian guard** suggests that he was jailed in their barracks. Paul the evangelist is at work even in this context, for the entire Praetorian guard knew that he was in prison because of Christ (Phil 1:13).

All of Paul's letters, in common with the Hellenistic letter of the day, conclude with a wish for the well-being of his readers, somewhat like our: "Take care." In the Hellenistic letter "fare-thee-well," which combined "goodbye" and a wish for good health, was pretty much standard. Paul's closing wish, on the other hand, has a decidedly spiritual focus. With little variation, he concludes virtually every letter with: "The grace of the Lord Jesus Christ be with you." Philippians, however, is distinctive in adding **be with your spirit**. "The grace of our Lord Jesus Christ" was spelled out by Paul in chapter 2:5–8. He laid aside his heavenly privileges, took on the form of a human being, and became a servant even unto death on a cross.

BIBLIOGRAPHY

Abrahamsen, Valerie. 1988. "Christianity and the Rock Reliefs at Philippi." *BA* 51:46–56.

Bakirtzis, Charalambos and Helmut Koester, eds. 1998. *Philippi at the Time of Paul and after His Death*. Harrisburg: Trinity Press International.

Bakken, Norman K. 1968. "The New Humanity: Christ and the Modern Age, A Study Centering in the Christ-Hymn: Phil. 2:6–11." *Int* 22:71–82.

Bandstra, Andrew J. 1966. "'Adam' and 'the Servant' in Phil. 2:5–11." *CTJ* 1:213–16.

Barclay, William. 1954. *The Letters to the Corinthians*. Edinburgh: St. Andrew Press.

———. 2003. *The Letters to the Philippians, Colossians, and Thessalonians*. 3rd ed. Louisville: Westminster/John Knox.

Bauer, Walter, et al. 2000. *A Greek-English Lexicon of the New Testament and Other Early Christian Literature*. 3rd ed. Chicago: University of Chicago Press.

Beare, F.W. 1973. *A Commentary on the Epistle to the Philippians*. 3rd ed. HNTC. New York: Harper & Row.

Belleville, Linda. 1987. "Continuity or Discontinuity: A Fresh Look at I Corinthians in Light of First Century Epistolary Forms and Conventions." *EQ* 59 (1987) 15–37.

———. 1996. *2 Corinthians*. Downers Grove, IL: InterVarsity.

Bird, Michael. 2009. *Colossians and Philemon. A New Covenant Commentary*. Eugene, OR: Cascade.

Best, Ernest. 1968. "Bishops and Deacons: Philippians 1:1." *SE* 4:371–76.

Black, David A. 1985. "Paul and Christian Unity: A Formal Analysis of Philippians 2:1–4." *JETS* 28:299–308.

———. 1995. "The Discourse Structure of Philippians: A Study in Textlinguistics." *NovT* 37:16–49.

Blass, F., et al. 1961. *A Greek Grammar of the New Testament and Other Early Christian Literature*. 9th ed. Chicago: University of Chicago Press.

Bockmuehl, Markus. 1997. "'The Form of God' (Phil 2:6): Variations on a Theme of Jewish Mysticism." *JETS* 48:1–23.

———. 1998. *The Epistle to the Philippians*. BNTC 11. Peabody, MA: Hendrickson.

Bornkamm, Gunther. 1959. "Zum Verständnis des Christus-Hymnus, Phil. 2:6–11." In *Studien zu Antike und Urchristentum*, 177–87. München: Kaiser.

Boyer, C. 1979. "Une étude sur le texte de l'épître aux Philippiens 2, 6–11." *DC* 32:5–14.

Brewer, Raymone R. 1954. "The Meaning of *Politeuesthe* in Philippians 1:27." *JBL* 73:76–83.

Brown, Truesdell S. 1958, . *Timaeus of Tauromenium*. Berkeley: University of California Press.

Bruce, Frederick F. 1989. *Philippians*. NICNT. Peabody, MA: Hendrickson.

Buchanan C. D. 1964. "Epaphroditus' Sickness and the Letter to the Philippians." *EvQ* 36: 157–66.

Bultmann, Rudolf. 1951. *Theology of the New Testament*. 2 vols. New York: Scribner's.

Burton, Ernest de Witt. 1896. "The Epistles of the Imprisonment." *BW* 7:46–56.

Byzantine Catholic Church. 2006. *The Divine Liturgies of our Holy Fathers John Chysostom and Basil the Great*. https://mci.archpitt.org/liturgy/Divine_Liturgy.html.

Cassidy, Richard J. 2001. *Paul in Chains: Roman Imprisonment and the Letters of Paul*. New York: Crossroad.

Collange, Jean-François. 1979. *The Epistle of Saint Paul to the Philippians*. Translated by A. W. Heathcote. London: Epworth.

Cousar, Charles B. 2009. *Philippians and Philemon: A Commentary*. NTL. Louisville: Westminster/John Knox.

Cowan, Ross. 2014. *Roman Guardsman, 62 BC—AD 324*. Oxford: Oxford University Press.

Craddock, Fred B. 1985. *Philippians*. IBC. Atlanta: John Knox.

Cross, F. L., ed. 2005. "Clement of Rome, St." In *The Oxford Dictionary of the Christian Church*. New York: Oxford University Press.

Croy, N. Clayton. 2003. "'To Die Is Gain' (Philippians 1:19–26): Does Paul Contemplate Suicide?" *JBL* 122:517–31.

Culpepper, R. Alan. 1980. "Co-Workers in Suffering: Philippians 2:19–30." *RevExp* 77:349–58.

Dahl, Nils A. 1995. "Euodia and Syntyche and Paul's Letter to the Philippians." In *The Social World of the First Christians: Essays in Honor of Wayne A. Meeks*, edited by L. Michael White and O. Larry Yarbrough, 3–15. Minneapolis: Fortress.

Dalton, W. J. 1979. "The Integrity of Philippians." *Bib* 60:97–102.

Dawe, D. G. 1962. "A Fresh look at the Kenotic Christologies." *SJT* 15:337–49.

De la Bédoyère, Guy. 2017. *Praetorian: The Rise and Fall of Rome's Imperial Bodyguard*. New Haven, CT: Yale University Press.

Dibelius, Martin. 1915. "ἁρπαγμός, Phil. 2, 6." *TLZ* 40:557–58.

Doble, Peter. 2003. "'Vile Bodies' or Transformed Persons? Philippians 3.21 in Context." *JSNT* 86:3–27.

Dodd, C. H. 1953. *New Testament Studies*. Manchester: Manchester University Press.

Doty, William G. 1973. *Letters in Primitive Christianity*. Minneapolis: Fortress.

Droge, Arthur J. 1988. "*Mori Lucrum*: Paul and Ancient Theories of Suicide." *NovT* 30:263–86.

Duncan, G. S. 1929. *St. Paul's Ephesian Ministry*. New York: Scribners.

———. 1955–1956. "Were Paul's Imprisonment Epistles Written from Ephesus?" *ExpTim* 67:163–66.

Dunn, James. 2003. *Christology in the Making. Inquiry Into the Origins of the Doctrine of the Incarnation*. 3rd ed. London: SCM.

Dupont, J. 1950. "Jésus-Christ dans son abaissement et son exaltation d'après Phil. II 6–11." *RSR* 37:500–514.

Eckman, Barbara. 1980. "A Quantitative Metrical Analysis of the Philippians Hymn." *NTS* 26:258–66.

Edwards, Mark J., ed. 1999. *Galatians, Ephesians, and Philippians*. ACCS 8. Downers Grove, IL: InterVarsity.

Eisenberg, Ronald L. 2015. *The 613 Mitzvot: A Contemporary Guide to the Commandments of Judaism*. Rockville, MD: Schreiber.

Engberg-Pedersen, Troels. 2003. "Radical Altruism in Philippians 2:4." In *Early Christianity and Classical Culture: Comparative Studies in Honor of Abraham J. Malherbe*, edited by John Fitzgerald et al., 197–214. Leiden: Brill.

Encyclopedia Britannica Online. 2008."Roman Citizenship." https://www.britannica.com/topic/civitas.

———2019."Hymn."http://0-www.search.eb.com.library.uor.edu:80/eb/ article-9041781.

Fee, Gordon D. 1992. "Philippians 2:5–11: Hymn or Exalted Pauline Prose?" *BBR* 2:29–46.

———. 1995. *Paul's Letter to the Philippians*. NICNT. Rev. ed. Grand Rapids: Eerdmans.

———. 1998. "To What End Exegesis? Reflections on Exegesis and Spirituality in Philippians 4:10–20." *BBR* 8:75–88.

———. 1999. *Philippians*. IVPNTC. Downers Grove, IL: InterVarsity.

Feuillet, A. 1965. "L'hymne christologique de l'épître aux Philippiens." *RB* 72:352–80; 481–507.

Finley, Michael B. 1973. "The Spirit of Kenōsis." *BT* 69:389–94.

Fowl, Stephen E. 1990. *The Story of Christ in the Ethics of Paul: An Analysis of the Function of the Hymnic Material in the Pauline Corpus*. JSNTSup. 36. Sheffield: JSOT.

Friberg, Barbara, et al. 2005. *Analytical Lexicon of the Greek New Testament*. Bloomington, IN: Trafford.

Furness, J. M. 1958–1959. "The Authorship of Phil ii, 6–11." *ExpTim* 70:240–43.

———. 1967–1968. "Behind the Philippians Hymn." *ExpTim* 79:178–82.

Garland, David E. 1985. "The Composition and Unity of Philippians: Some Neglected Literary Factors." *NovT* 27:141–73.

Georgi, D. 1964. "Der vorpaulinische Hymnus Phil 2,6–11." In *Zeit und Geschichte. Dankesgabe an Rudolf Bultmann zum 80. Geburtstag*, edited by E. Dinkler. Tübingen: Mohr.

Gibbs, John G. 1971. "Philippians 2:6–11." In *Creation and Redemption. A Study in Pauline Theology*. NovTSup 26. Leiden: Brill.

Glasson, T. Francis. 1974–1975. "Two Notes on the Philippians Hymn (ii..6—11)." *NTS* 21:133–39.

Gorman, Michael J. 2009. *Inhabiting the Cruciform God: Kenosis, Justification, and Theosis in Paul's Narrative Soteriology*. Grand Rapids: Eerdmans.

Gove, Philip B. 1993. *Webster's Third New International Dictionary of the English Language*. Springfield, MA: Encyclopedia Britannica.

Greenlee, J. Harold. 1986. *A Concise Exegetical Grammar of New Testament Greek*. Grand Rapids: Eerdmans.

Gundry, Robert. 1994. "Style and Substance in 'the Myth of God Incarnate' According to Philippians 2:6–11." In *Crossing the Boundaries. Essays in Biblical Interpretation in Honor of Michael Goulder*, edited by Stanley Porter, et al., 271–93. Leiden: Brill.

Hagelberg, Dave. 2007. *Philippians: An Ancient Thank You Letter—A Study of Paul and His Ministry Partners' Relationship*. Manila: Philippine Challenge.

Hammerich, L. L. 1967. "An Ancient Misunderstanding (Phil. 2,6 'robbery'). *ExpTim* 78:193–94.

Hansen, G. Walter. 2009. *The Letter to the Philippians*. PNTC. Grand Rapids: Eerdmans.

Harvey, John. 1965. "A New Look at the Christ Hymn in Philippians 2:6–11." *ExpTim* 76:338.

Havlicek, Filip, and Miroslav Morcineck. 2016. "Waste and Pollution in the Ancient Roman Empire." *Journal of Landscape Ecology* 9:33–49.

Hawthorne, Gerald F. 1983. *Philippians*. WBC 43. Waco, TX: Word.

Hellerman, Joseph H. 2005. *Reconstructing Honor in Roman Philippi: Carmen Christi as Cursus Pudorum*. SNTSMS 132. Cambridge: Cambridge University Press.

Helmbold, A. K. 1974. "Redeemer Hymns—Gnostic and Christian." In *New Dimensions in New Testament Study*, edited by R. N. Longenecker and M. C. Tenney. Grand Rapids: Zondervan.

Hofius, O. 1976. *Der Christushymnus Philipper 2, 6–11*. WUNT 17. Tübingen: J. C. B. Mohr.

Holloway, Paul A. 2001. *Consolation in Philippians: Philosophical Sources and Rhetorical Strategy*. SNTSMS 112. Cambridge: Cambridge University Press.

Hooker, Morna D. 1975. "Philippians 2:6–11." In *Jesus and Paulus: Festschrift fur Werner Georg Kümmel zum 70*, edited by Earle Ellis and Erich Grässer, 151–64. Göttingen: Vandenhoeck & Ruprecht.

Howard, George. 1978. "Phil. 2:6–11 and the Human Christ." *CBQ* 40:368–87.

Hudson, D. F. 1965-1966. "A Further Note on Philippians ii.6–11." *ExpTim* 77:29.

Hurtado, Larry. 1984. "Jesus as Lordly Example in Philippians 2:5–11." In *From Jesus to Paul: Studies in Honour of Francis Wright Beare*, edited by P. Richardson and J.C. Hurd, 113–26. Waterloo, ON: Wilfrid Laurier.

Jeremias, Joachim. 1963. "Zu Phil. ii 7: EAYTON EKENΩΣEN." *NovT* 6:182–88.

Jervell, J. 1960. *Imago Dei. Gen. 1.26f im Spätjudentum, in der Gnosis und in den paulinischen Briefen*. FRLANT 63. Göttingen: Vandenhoeck & Ruprecht.

Jewett, Robert. 1970. "The Epistolary Thanksgiving and the Integrity of Philippians." *NovT* 12:40–53.

Johnson, Lewis. 1957-58. "The Pauline Letters from Caesarea." *ExpTim* 68:24–26.

Käsemann, Ernst. 1968. "A Critical Analysis of Philippians 2:5–11." *JTC* 5:45–88.

Kelly, John N. D. 2006. *Early Christian Creeds*. 3rd ed. London/New York: Continuum.

Kent, Homer A., Jr. 1978. *Philippians*. EBC 11. Grand Rapids: Zondervan.

Kittel, G., and G. Friedrich, eds. 1964-1976. *Theological Dictionary of the New Testament*. 10 vols. Translated by G. W. Bromiley. Grand Rapids: Eerdmans.

Knox, W. L. 1948. "The 'Divine-Hero' Christology in the New Testament." *HTR* 41:229–49.

Lambrecht, Jan. 2003. "The Identity of Christ Jesus (Philippians 2, 6–11)." In *Understanding What One Reads: New Testament Essays*, edited by Veronica Kopersky, 245–62. Leuven: Peeters.

Lanciani, Rodolfo A. 1890. *Ancient Rome in the Light of Recent Discoveries*. Boston: Houghton Mifflin.

Lemerle, P. 1945. *Philippes et la Macédoine orientale à l'époque chrétienne et byzantine*. Paris: E. de Boccard.

Lenski, R. C. H. 1937. *The Interpretation of St. Paul's Epistles to the Galatians, to the Ephesians, and to the Philippians*. Repr. ed. Peabody, MA: Hendrickson, 2001.

Liddell, H. G., et al. 1996. *A Greek-English Lexicon with a Revised Supplement*. 9th ed. New York: Oxford University Press.

Lightfoot, J. B. 1953. *St. Paul's Epistle to the Philippians: A Revised Text with Introduction, Notes, and Dissertations*. 4th ed. London: Macmillan.

Lisco, Heinrich. 1900. *Vincula Sanctorum. Ein Beitrag zur Erklärung der Gefangenschaftsbriefe des Apostels Paulus*. Berlin: Schneider.

Llewelyn, Stephen R. 1995. "Sending Letters in the Ancient World: Paul and the Philippians." *TynBul* 46:337–56.

Lohmeyer, Ernst. 1928. *Kyrios Jesus; eine Untersuchung zu Phil. 2,5–11*. Philosophisch-Historische Klasse 18. Heidelberg: C. Winter.

Longenecker, Richard. 1970. *The Christology of Early Jewish Christianity*. London: SCM.

Losie, L. A. 1978. "A Note on the Interpretation of Phil. 2:5." *ExpTim* 90:52–54.

Louw, J. P., and E. A. Nida. 1988–1989. *Greek-English Lexicon of the New Testament*. 2 vols. New York: United Bible Society.

Mackay, B. S. 1960–61. "Further Thoughts on Philippians." *NTS* 7:161–70.

MacQuarrie, John. 1974. "Kenoticism Reconsidered." *Theology* 77:11–24.

Marshall, I. Howard. 1968. "The Christ-Hymn in Philippians 2:5–11." *TynBul* 19:104–27.

Martin, Dale B. 1996. "The Construction of the Ancient Family: Methodological Considerations." *JRS* 86:40–60.

Martin, R. P. 1959–60. "*Morphē* in Philippians ii.6." *ExpTim* 70:183–84.

———. 1960. *An Early Christian Confession. Philippians 2:5–11 in Recent Interpretation*. London: Tyndale.

———. 1964. "The Form-Analysis of Philippians 2.5–11." *TU* 87:611–20.

———. 1967. *Carmen Christi. Philippians 2:5–11 in Recent Interpretation and in the Setting of Early Christian Worship*. Cambridge: Cambridge University Press.

———. 1975. *Worship in the Early Church*. Rev. ed. Grand Rapids: Eerdmans.

———. 1980. *Philippians*. NCB. Grand Rapids: Eerdmans.

———. 1987. *The Epistle of Paul to the Philippians: An Introduction and Commentary*. TNTC. Rev. ed. Grand Rapids: Eerdmans.

———. 1997. *A Hymn of Christ: Philippians 2:5–11 in Recent Interpretation and in the Setting of Early Christian Worship*. Downers Grove, IL: InterVarsity.

Martin, Ralph P. and Gerald F. Hawthorne. 2004. *Philippians*. Rev. ed. WBC 43. Nashville: Nelson.

McAlister, Bryan. 2011. "Introduction to Philippians: Mindful of How We Fill Our Minds." *Gospel Advocate* 153:12–13.

McClain, Alva J. 1998. "The Doctrine of the Kenōsis in Philippians 2:5–8." *The Master's Seminary Journal* 9:85–96.

McNeile, A. H. 1995. *An Introduction to the New Testament*. Oxford: Oxford University Press.

Meeks, Wayne A. 1991. "The Man from Heaven in Philippians." In *The Future of Christianity in Honor of H. Koester*, edited by Birger A. Pearson, 329–36. Minneapolis: Fortress.

Melick, Richard R. 1991. *Philippians, Colossians, Philemon*. NAC 34. Nashville: Broadman.

Mirbt, Carl Theodor. 1911. "Nicaea, Council of." In *Encyclopedia Britannica* 19, edited by Hugh Chisholm, 640–42. Cambridge: Cambridge University Press.

Moule, C. F. D. 1953. *An Idiom Book of New Testament Greek*. Cambridge: Cambridge University Press.

———. 1970. "Further Reflexions on Phil. 2:5–11." In *Apostolic History and the Gospel*, edited by W. Ward Gasque and Ralph P. Martin, 266. Grand Rapids: Eerdmans.

Moule, H. C. G. 1908. *Philippian Studies*. 6th ed. London: Hodder & Stoughton.

Moulton, James, and George Milligan. 1929. *The Vocabulary of the Greek Testament, Illustrated from the papyri and other non-literary sources*. Grand Rapids: Eerdmans.

Müller, Jacobus J. 1955. *The Epistle of Paul to the Philippians*. NICNT. Grand Rapids: Eerdmans.

Murphy-O'Connor, J. 1976. "Christological Anthropology in Phil. 2:6–11." *RB* 83:25–50.

Neufeld, V. H. 1963. *The Earliest Christian Confessions*. NTTS 5. Leiden: Brill.

Oakes, Peter. 2001. *Philippians: From People to Letter*. SNTSMS 110. Cambridge: Cambridge University Press.

O'Brien, Peter, T. 1991. *The Epistle to the Philippians—A Commentary on the Greek Text*. Grand Rapids: Eerdmans.

Osiek, Carolyn. 2000. *Philippians, Philemon*. ANTC. Nashville: Abingdon.

O'Toole, Robert F. 1996. "Slave Girl at Philippi." In *The Anchor Bible Dictionary*, edited by N. Freedman 6:57–58. New York: Doubleday.

Peppard, Michael. 2008. "Poetry, Hymns, and Traditional Material in the New Testament Epistles." *NTS* 30:319–42.

Peterlin, Davorin. 1995. *Paul's Letter to the Philippians in the Light of Disunity in the Church*. NovTSup 79. Leiden: Brill.

Peterman, G. W. 1997. *Paul's Gift from Philippi: Conventions of Gift-Exchange and Christian Giving*. SNTSMS 92. Cambridge: Cambridge University Press.

Plummer, A. 1919. *A Commentary on St. Paul's Epistle to the Philippians*. London: Robert Scott Roxburghe.

Portefaix, Lillian. 1988. *Sisters Rejoice: Paul's Letter to the Philippians and Luke-Acts as Seen by First-Century Philippian Women*. CBNTS 20. Stockholm: Almquist & Wiksell.

Reicke, Bo. 1970. "Caesarea, Rome, and the Captivity Epistles." In *Apostolic History and the Gospel. Biblical and Historical Essays Presented to F. F. Bruce on His 60th Birthday*, edited by Ward Gasque and R. P. Martin, 277–86. Grand Rapids: Eerdmans.

Reiher, Jim. 2012. "Could Philippians have been written from the Second Roman Imprisonment?" *EvQ* 84:213–33.

Reitzenstein, R. 1978. *Hellenistic Mystery Religions*. Translated by J. E. Steely. PTMS 15. Pittsburg: Pickwick.

Reumann, John H. P. 2008. "Philippians." *AB* 33B. New Haven, CT: Yale University Press.

Schweitzer, Albert. 1953. *The Mysticism of Paul the Apostle*. Baltimore: John's Hopkins University.

Sergio, Rosell Nebreda. 2011. *Christ Identity: A Social-Scientific Reading of Philippians 2.5–11*. Göttingen: Vandenhoeck & Ruprecht.

Shaner, Katherine A. 2017. "Seeing Rape and Robbery: ἁρπαγμός; and the Philippians Christ Hymn (Phil. 2:5–11)." *BibInt* 25:342–63.

Sharp, Granville. 1803. *Remarks on the Uses of the Definitive Article in the Greek Text of the New Testament: Containing Many New Proofs of the Divinity of Christ, from Passages Which Are Wrongly Translated in the Common English Version*. 3rd ed. London: Verner and Hood: Introduction.

Silva, Moisés. 2005. *Philippians*. 2nd ed. BECNT. Grand Rapids: Baker Academic.

Smith, William. 1875. "Praetoriani." *A Dictionary of Greek and Roman Antiquities*. John Murray: London.

Still, Todd D. 2011. *Philippians and Philemon*. Smyth & Helwys Bible Commentaries 27b. Macon, GA: Smyth & Helwys.

Streiker, L. D. 1964. "The Christological Hymn in Phil 2." *LQ* 16:49–58.

Strimple, Robert. 1979. "Philippians 2:5–11 in Recent Studies: Some Exegetical Conclusions." *WTJ* 41:247–68.

Swaddling, Judith. 2000. *The Ancient Olympic Games*. 2nd ed. University of Texas Press.

Talbert, C. H. 1967. "The Problem of Pre-existence in Phil. 2:6–11." *JBL* 86:141–53.

Thielman, Frank. 1995. *Philippians*. NIVAC. Grand Rapids: Zondervan.

Thomas, J. 1975. "L'hymnè de l'Epître aux Philippiens." *Christus* 22:334–45.

Thomas, T. A. 1970. "The Kenōsis Question." *EvQ* 42:142–51.

Thurston, Bonnie B. 2005. "Philippians." In *Philippians and Philemon*, 1–163. Collegeville, MN: Liturgical.

van der Crabben, Jan. 2009–2019. *Ancient History Encyclopedia*. Horsham: UK.

Versnel, H. S. 1998. *Transition and Reversal in Myth and Ritual*. Leiden: Brill.

Vincent, M. R. 1897. *A Critical and Exegetical Commentary on the Epistles to the Philippians and Philemon*. ICC. Edinburgh: T. & T. Clark.

Vögtle, A. 1936. *Die Tugend- und Lasterkataloge im Neuen Testament*. Münster: W. Aschendorff.

Wannamaker, C. A. 1987. "Philippians 2.6–11: Son of God or Adamic Christology?" *NTS* 33:179–93.

Wansink, Craig S. 1996. *Chained in Christ: The Experience and Rhetoric of Paul's Imprisonments*. JSNTSup. 130. Sheffield: Sheffield Academic.

Ware, James P. 2005. *The Mission of the Church in Paul's Letter to the Philippians in the Context of Ancient Judaism*. NovTSup. 120. Leiden: Brill.

Wesley, John. 1738. *A Plain Account of Christian Perfection*. London.

White, John. 1971. "Introductory Formulae in the Body of the Pauline Letters." *JBL* 90:74–82.

———. 1972. *The Form and Function of the Body of the Greek Letter: A Study of the Letter Body in the Non-Literary Papyri and in Paul the Apostle*. SBLDS 2. Missoula: Scholars Press.

———. 1986. *Light From Ancient Letters*. Minneapolis: Fortress.

Wilson, R. E. 1976. "He Emptied Himself." *JETS* 19:279–81.

Wibbing, S. 1959. *Die Tugend und Lasterkataloge im Neuen Testament. und ihre Traditionsgeschichte unter besonderer Berücksichtigung der Qumran-Texte*. BZNW 25. Berlin: Alfred Töpelmann.

Wood, J. T. 1877. *Discoveries at Ephesus*. London: Longmans, Green.

Wright, N. T. 1986. "ἁρπαγμός and the Meaning of Philippians 2:5–11." *JTS* 37:321–52.

———. 1992. *The Climax of the Covenant: Christ and the Law in Pauline Theology*. Edinburgh: T. & T. Clark.